Build your own rainbow

A WORKBOOK
FOR CAREER AND
LIFE MANAGEMENT
by
Dr Barrie Hopson
and Mike Scally

MERCURY

First published in 1984 by
Lifeskills Publishing Group

New Edition published in May 1991
by Mercury Books
Gold Arrow Publications Limited
862 Garratt Lane, London SW17 0NB

Reprinted November 1991
Reprinted November 1992

Set in 9/11 pt Helvetica by TecSet Ltd, Wallington, Surrey.
Printed in Great Britain by
Dotesios Ltd, Trowbridge, Wiltshire

British Library Cataloguing in Publication Data
Hopson, Barrie
  Build you own rainbow: A workbook for career and life
  management. – (Lifeskills for adults)
  I. Title II. Scally, Michael III. Series
  650.14

ISBN 1–85252–074–4

A Workbook for
Career and Life Management

DR BARRIE HOPSON

MIKE SCALLY

Barrie is Joint Managing Director of Lifeskills Management Group and co-founder of Lifeskills Communications Ltd. Previously he founded the Counselling and Career Development Unit at Leeds University and was the first Director until 1984. He has worked widely as a consultant to industrial and educational organisations in the UK, USA and Europe. He was responsible for setting up the first career counselling service in British industry in 1970 (at ICI) and has since helped a number of organisations in different countries to set up career counselling and career management systems. He is a professional Associate of the National Training Laboratories for Applied Behavioral Science in Washington DC, a Fellow of the British Psychological Society and of the British Institute of Management.

He has written 22 books and numerous articles on personal and career development, marriage, lifeskills teaching, quality service, transition and change management and generic training skills.

Mike is Joint Managing Director of Lifeskills Management Group. He combines management training with writing and lecturing. He was Deputy Director of the Counselling and Career Development Unit at Leeds University in 1976 and was involved with its training programmes and national projects until 1984.

He has an extensive experience of training in many of the UK's major companies and an international reputation in the field of education. He serves on the management committees of, and is consultant to, many national groups – promoting development education and training at home and abroad.

Mike Scally has written 12 books and many articles on career management, customer services and lifeskills teaching.

Acknowledgements

This book represents 15 years of work and development. It took only months to write but those 15 years are written into every page. We have found that the rationale and the techniques it contain have been of immense value to us personally and that experience has been echoed by the thousands of people who have also experienced the career and life management programmes, which form the basis of the book.

There are many special acknowledgements we wish to make:

- to Valerie Maunder of Lifeskills Management Group who has provided the up-to-date occupational information
- to Lorna Bailey of the Open University who, with help from Monica Darlington, Mick Jones and Nick Farnes, taught us so much about translating a workshop into a written format
- to Jen Anderson, John Bennett, Jackie Bould, Peter Eastwood, Judith Stewart, of the Counselling and Career Development Unit for valuable feedback
- to Florence Lewis of Bank America, California, Jack Loughary of the University of Oregon, Dick Knowdell of Career Testing and Design, San Jose, and Donald Super of Teachers College, Columbia University for ideas, suggestions and feedback
- to Hobson's Press for permission to reproduce the self-employment questionnaire from 'Your Own Business'
- to Sidgwick and Jackson for permission to reproduce the life satisfactions figure from Gail Sheehy's "Pathfinders"
- to everyone who has participated and contributed to all of those workshops over 15 years and who thereby have helped us to build our rainbow
- to more than 150 development testers of the Open University who piloted the materials.

This book is significant for us both in another, very relevant way. Both our careers have been characterised by the cyclical career pattern (see page 1). When we wrote the first edition of this book in 1984, we had just resigned from our full-time posts as Director and Deputy Director of the Counselling and Career Development Unit at Leeds University to form Lifeskills Associates. We had spent eight marvellous years building that particular rainbow.

As we prepare this new edition, we have just split Lifeskills Associates into two companies: Lifeskills Management Group, an international joint venture with the Hay Group (the world's largest human resources consulting group) and Lifeskills Communications. Rainbows do not last forever, even ones you build yourself. As one begins to fade, another is waiting to be built. Our two new companies are our current rainbows – at least for a while.

Be a Rainbow Builder – you *can* manage your life and your career. This book is an invitation to begin now.

Barrie Hopson and Mike Scally

Leeds, September 1990

CONTENTS

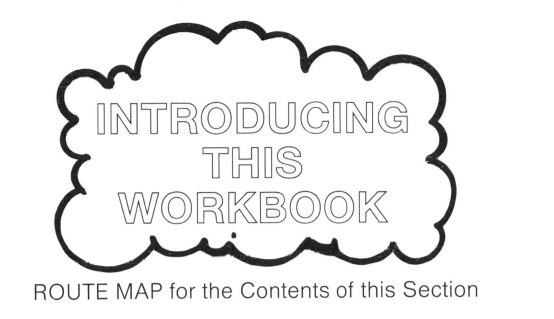

INTRODUCING THIS WORKBOOK

ROUTE MAP for the Contents of this Section

You are here

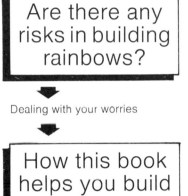

Build your own rainbow now

You can take charge of your life
The process of career and life management
Why build your own rainbow?

What does a rainbow builder need to do?

The 6 basic questions of career and life management
7 skills you will need to develop

Where are you starting from?

Take a look at your life
What do you want to be different or better about your life?

Are there any risks in building rainbows?

Dealing with your worries

How this book helps you build your rainbow

The exercises
Route map
Questions
Watchpoints
Facts
Quotations
Keeping your notes
Working with a partner
Checking your progress
Timing

Building a contract with this book.

Build Your Own Rainbow Now!

"Here is Edward Bear, coming downstairs now, bump, bump, on the back of his head behind Christopher Robin. It is, as far as he knows, the only way of coming downstairs, but sometimes he feels there really is another way, if only he could stop bumping for a moment and think of it."

A. A. Milne, Winnie the Pooh

Edward Bear's experience is, unfortunately, not totally unfamiliar to most of us at times. We may be aware of a vague dissatisfaction or perhaps even a major problem. We worry, we feel anxious, we do not seem to be getting anywhere. Indeed, we are not sure just where we would like to get to or even how to recognise that we have arrived. That is exactly the time to "stop our world" and to get off; to examine our lives from the outside and ourselves from the inside.

There is a game people often play with themselves called:

"It will be different when...."

- I've passed my exams
- I've left school
- I've got my promotion
- I've changed jobs
- I'm married
- We've got children
- The children leave home
- I retire..."

Does this sound familiar to you?

If we are not careful, the months, and then the years can go by as we wait and yet never really take charge of our own lives. The habit of waiting for things to happen can develop early in life. Hence, it is early in life that we need to begin to believe and to demonstrate that:

THERE IS ALWAYS AN ALTERNATIVE

TOMORROW NEED NOT BE LIKE TODAY

THINGS DO NOT HAVE TO BE GOING BADLY BEFORE THEY CAN GET BETTER

Each of us has 168 hours to live each week. For a 30 year old with an average life expectancy of 75 years that equals a total of 393,120 hours left to live.

With such a huge investment of time — an ever decreasing resource, it seems not unreasonable to ask ourselves:

"What return am I getting currently on the way I am spending my time?"

"What return do I want?"

"At the end of my life, what will I need to have done to be able to say to myself, 'that was the best way I could have invested those hours'?"

You can take charge of your life.

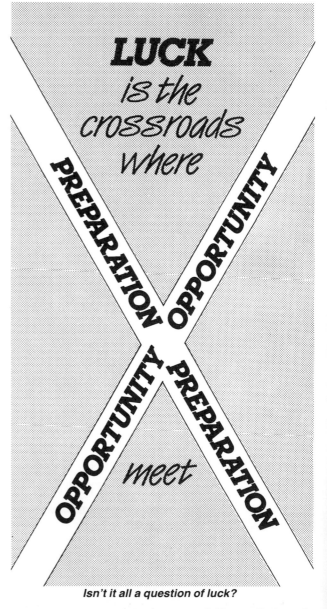

LUCK is the crossroads where PREPARATION OPPORTUNITY OPPORTUNITY PREPARATION OPPORTUNITY PREPARATION meet

Isn't it all a question of luck?

Clearly, accidents in life happen to us all. There will always be factors over which we have little or no control, but, in our experience, many people ascribe good or bad things that happen to them to fate, and minimise their own contributions to events.

Pinball living or self-empowerment?

Elsewhere[1] we have written about the dissatisfactions that flow from what we call 'pinball-living'.

Balls in a pinball machine have no life of their own; they are set in motion by someone else and then bounce from one place to another without any clear direction, sometimes even making big scores, but then sinking into oblivion until someone sets them off again.

The opposite to pinball living is self-empowered living

Self-empowerment is a process by which we increasingly take greater charge of ourselves and our lives. To operate in a self-empowered way entails being able to:

- believe that, and operate in the belief that, we are open to and able to change;

- have the skills to change some aspects of ourselves and the world in which we live;

- use our feelings to recognise where there is a discrepancy between the way things are and the way we would like them to be;

- specify desired outcomes and the action steps required to achieve them;

- act – to implement our action plans;

- live each day being aware of our power to assess, review, influence and self-direct;

- help others to become more self-empowered.

To become more self-empowered we need to know:

"What is important to me in life"

"What I want to do with my life"

"What beliefs will help me to get what I want"

"What information I need about myself and our world"

"What skills I need to get me what I want"

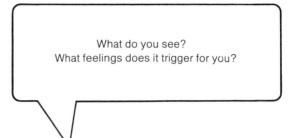

These are the building blocks for personal change.

Why 'build your own rainbow'?

A rainbow throughout history has been a symbol of hope and achievement. In China it is viewed as the bridge between this world and paradise. In India it represents the highest attainable yogic state. In our every day Western world it is often viewed as ephemeral and beautiful, beautiful perhaps partly because of its ephemerality.

What do you think of when you think about rainbows?

Sit back, close your eyes. Picture a rainbow.

> What do you see?
> What feelings does it trigger for you?

We have chosen to build this book around a rainbow because to many people it represents hope, beauty, and optimism. Career and life management is a process that can enable each of us to make our lives more like we want them to be.

We depart, however, from the traditional symbol in believing that we do not have to wait for the elements to meet by chance to provide us with our personal rainbows. We can build our own rainbows. They are within the grasp of each of us.

Another part of rainbow mythology is the famed pot of gold which can be found where the rainbow touches the earth. People who try to find the elusive pot of gold by chasing rainbows are often called day-dreamers or idealists with their heads in the clouds due to their habit of hoping for impossible things. And we would agree – to a point.

There is little gain from hoping for impossible things, but planning is the best way we know of converting the impossible into the realm of the possible.

Perhaps the "rainbow-chasers" make their mistakes in assuming that the pots of gold are "out there" somewhere, waiting to be found.

The true "rainbow-builders" know that the treasure lies within themselves waiting to be moulded and formed into images constrained largely only by the limits of their own imaginations.

The RAINBOW is the vision. The tools we need to build our rainbows are our *skills*. The clouds on the horizon are necessary *questions* we need to answer before we can build our rainbows.

Be a Rainbow-Builder Not a Rainbow Chaser

For a number of years we and our colleagues at Lifeskills have been helping thousands of adults to "build their own rainbows" in workshops in the UK, USA, Sweden, Holland and Ireland. These workshops, typically, have been for employees within organisations which have asked us to help them introduce the concept of self-managed careers into their organisational cultures. We have run them for senior management, middle management, supervisory and operative levels; for industry, commerce, the health services, social services, universities and for some Local Education Authority staffs. We have run workshops for married couples, religious groups, for secondary school staff and for youth services. We give you this roll-call not to impress you with the amount of work done but to underline how widely these techniques can be used. The principles have now been transferred into a teaching programme for young people aged 14–19 years.[2]

What Does a Rainbow Builder Need To Do?

The 6 clouds represent the 6 basic questions of career and life management. These are in logical sequence:

1. Who am I?

- What are my transferable skills, my values, my interests?
- How do I spend my time?
- Where do I want to live and work?

2. Where am I now?

- Which stage of life am I at?
- What kind of career pattern do I want?

3. How satisfied am I?

This will involve an analysis of all my important life roles: child, student, employee, friend, consumer, citizen, leisure-user, homemaker, and, where appropriate – spouse and parent.

4. What changes do I want?

A perfectly legitimate answer can be "none". This does not render the earlier questions useless. What can happen through reviewing our lives is that we may discover that we really like much of what they contain. Reviewing our lives can provide new or renewed commitment to aspects of our present living. Many people on our adult workshops have returned revitalised to jobs, families, and lifestyle. They have discovered that they require to make some minor changes to their lives but that the major elements are fulfilling.

On the other hand, we have also witnessed some very dramatic changes. Adults have made decisions to change jobs, shift careers, get married or divorced, start a family, take up new interests, relinquish old ones. Some people discover that goals they had set for themselves years ago are no longer appropriate:

"I always thought that unless I became at least a production manager that I wouldn't have been successful, but that was what success meant to me in my twenties. It looks very different now I'm 43, so why am I still striving to get something that now I'm not sure I really want, and the striving is stopping me from enjoying what I've got."

Workshop participant

That quotation illustrates some of the benefits that can result from beginning to review our lives. Our own personal goals and needs may have stayed constant, but social changes can result in our being stuck with them, with the mainstream of social and technological development leaving us further behind.

"What happens when people invest a good part of their lives in a contract that society rewrites?"

Gail Sheehy,[3]

We may have to review not only our goals and behaviour, but beliefs that are fundamental to us but which now label us as a product of a former age.

We will also have to let our imaginations soar. There is a time for keeping one's feet on the ground but that only comes after we have soared to the limits of our imaginations. In rainbow-building we consciously encourage people to day-dream, to fantasise, to explore their ideals, to free themselves from the shackles of everyday life and its commitments.

"Your visions of the future are your assessments of the past."

Howard Figler,[4]

5. How do I make them happen?

Deciding what we want to change is the first vital step towards change. But, we all know that the road to hell is paved with good intentions. It is rarely paved with good objectives, because a good objective will lead us towards what we want to happen. The next step is to construct an action plan capable of achieving that objective. The final step is simply "to do it". That last step sounds the simplest but is sometimes the most difficult. It will be easier the better we become at objective setting and action planning. We may also need the help and support of other people to do this.

6. What if it doesn't work out?

However thorough our self-analysis, however brilliant our visions, however systematic our objectives and action plans, there is no guarantee that we can always build our rainbows as we want them when we want them.

How do we cope with the frustration and disappointment when things do not turn out as we wish them to?

This is where the "looking after yourself" skills are particularly crucial. A failed objective is simply that – a failed objective. It doesn't make *you* a failure. It simply means that your objective was unrealistic or not sufficiently well thought out. Failures need to be viewed more like undesirable computer feedback on a space-flight. It will be necessary to adjust course, or even abort the mission, but the promise of success will always have justified the attempt, and much will have been learned for future missions.

"Generally it is our failures that civilise us. Triumph confirms us in our habits."
Clive James,[5]

Skills You Will Need To Develop

Knowing Yourself
Learning From Experience
Research Skills
Setting Objectives & Making Action Plans
Making Decisions
Looking After Yourself
Communicating

A rainbow builder needs to have access to all 7 skills listed above.

This book will enable you to develop all of these skills. You will need to be looking after yourself throughout the process. You will frequently need to communicate with others, reassess your values and skills (knowing yourself), review what has happened (learning from experience), redefine your objectives, and consequently will need to find out more information (research skills) as a result of which new decisions will need to be made. We are offering you a process, based on the 6 career life management questions.

If you follow it, it will help you to find your own answers to what you want to do with your career and your life.

Let us examine the 7 skills in more detail

1. Knowing Yourself

To be a Rainbow-builder you need to have a thorough understanding of your raw materials, which in this case means you.

The analogy with building is not strictly accurate. Once objects are built their constitution and appearance stay primarily the same. You, however, are subject to change. Indeed, the very process of introspection and analysis will influence the person you are and will become.

For effective career and life management to take place you need to know how to get information on:

- *YOUR VALUES:* what is important to you in life?
- *YOUR TRANSFERABLE SKILLS:* what you can do and enjoy doing?
- *YOUR INTERESTS:* what activities are of interest to you irrespective of your skill levels?

However, you live within the context of the life you have built and that has developed around you. You need to know how to get information, therefore, on your present style of living:

- *HOW YOU PRESENTLY SPEND YOUR TIME:* what do you do, with whom, how often, for how long?

- *WHERE YOU LIVE*

- *AT WHICH LIFE STAGE YOU ARE:* do you know what life stages there are, and where you are in relation to them?

- *WHAT KIND OF CAREER PATTERN YOU WANT:* do you want one or a number of occupations? How many hours do you want to spend in paid work? How much variety do you need?

2. Learning from Experience

Some people never seem to learn from experience. They frequently seem to repeat mistakes. Why is that? We would argue that it stems from a failure to analyse an experience to see what can be learned from it. We call this process reviewing. It involves being able to:

- *DESCRIBE AN EXPERIENCE ONE HAS HAD*

- *IDENTIFY WHAT HAS BEEN LEARNED FROM IT*

- *GENERALISE THAT LEARNING TO OTHER SITUATIONS*

3. Research Skills

To obtain self-knowledge you need to develop the skills of looking inward, but the skills of accessing information outside of yourself are what we call research skills. You will need to know how to get information from:

- *KEY PEOPLE IN YOUR LIFE IN TERMS OF HOW THEY THINK YOU ARE DOING*

- *OTHER PEOPLE, PRINTED MATERIALS AND COMMUNITY RESOURCES*

4. Setting Objectives, Making Action Plans

A popular poster states:

"IF YOU DON'T KNOW WHERE YOU ARE GOING YOU'LL PROBABLY END UP SOMEWHERE ELSE"
David Campbell,[6]

Many people fail to get what they want in life because they have never worked out exactly what they do want. They experience dissatisfaction, they know something isn't right but they have never really developed the skill of converting complaints into aims, aims into objectives and objectives into action plans.

An *aim* is a general statement of what one wants to happen, e.g. ''I want a job''.

An *objective* is an aim made more specific, e.g. ''I want to get a job as a car mechanic''.

An *action plan* describes the steps that have to be completed before bringing that about.

Often prior to setting objectives we may need to let our imaginations soar to explore a wide range of possibilities.

Then we need to narrow down the possibilities.

The illustration below shows how this process occurs: always broaden the horizons and then narrow them down.

Some people do not find it easy to let their imaginations soar and need help to learn to do so.

Objective and action planning skills, therefore, involve knowing how to:

- *CONVERT YOUR COMPLAINTS INTO OBJECTIVES YOU WANT TO ACHIEVE*

- *FANTASISE FREELY*

- *DISCOVER THE PARTS OF YOUR LIFE YOU WISH TO CHANGE*

- *SET OBJECTIVES*

- *MAKE ACTION PLANS*

5. Making Decisions

The more information you collect about yourself and the world around you the easier it is to become paralysed by it.

The ability to generate alternative choices based upon the information, and having strategies for deciding between them is crucial.

6. Looking after Yourself

No-one has said that building rainbows is easy. Career and life management can be a demanding process.

Finding out about oneself can be very intellectually and emotionally testing. We can unearth aspects of ourselves that make us feel uncomfortable. We may be forced to face up to very 'crunchy' and challenging questions about how we are currently living our lives. At the end of the process, with our "Rainbows" carefully planned out, we might not be able to achieve our objectives. A vital skill, therefore, is to be able to look after oneself physically, rationally, and emotionally during the process and especially when things do not turn out as we had planned.

This involves being skilled in:

- *STRESS MANAGEMENT,* and

- *STRESS PREVENTION*

7. Communicating

Career and life management will always involve a considerable degree of working by oneself. The effective use of other people, however, will be crucial to the process. We need feedback from others. We have to ask for help and information. We have to be capable of expressing ourselves clearly, orally and on paper.

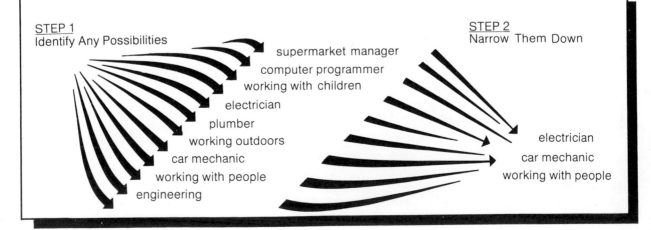

STEP 1
Identify Any Possibilities

supermarket manager
computer programmer
working with children
electrician
plumber
working outdoors
car mechanic
working with people
engineering

STEP 2
Narrow Them Down

electrician
car mechanic
working with people

Where Are You Starting From?

Your rainbow can be approached from one or many starting points.
This book offers a pathway to finding and building your rainbow. All the starting
points begin from a sense that "something might be different or better" in your life.

This can range in intensity from a feeling of major crisis to an interest in checking
out whether one is getting as much as one could out of life.

The following clouds all represent reasons commonly expressed
by people for coming to our career and life management workshops.

These could also be reasons for using this book.

I find it difficult to choose between the things that are important to me

I'm bored, apathetic, in a rut

I don't know what I want

I want to return to a job after bringing up my children

I want to be clearer about where I go from here in my career

I'm about to lose my job

I want to find out what's really important to me

I'm retiring soon and I don't know what to do

I'd like to learn to accept what I've got, to feel more at peace with myself

I'd like to know what jobs I'm capable of doing

I know what I want, but I don't know how to get it

I'm quite satisfied with my job at the moment, but I feel I may be missing out on something

List any others that might be true to you.

Write into the three clouds below your 3 most important reasons for using this book.

At the end of the book you will be reminded of these
and you will be asked whether this workbook
has helped you.

The hardest battle is to be nobody but yourself
in a world, which is doing its best, night and day, to make
you everybody else.

e. e. cummings

13

Take a look at your life

Lives, however hard we might try, cannot be completely compartmentalised. A job change is bound to affect other areas of your life. Changing a leisure habit may have consequences for how you spend your spare time and have an impact on your family life.

This book is designed to enable you to review your life as you are living it now, in total.

Let us examine some of the parts that together make up the whole that is YOUR LIFE.

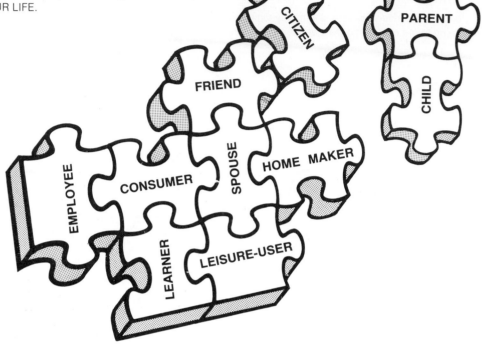

In the course of your lifetime you will occupy a variety of roles, like those in the jigsaw pieces. Sometimes they will connect with one another, at other times they will not and some will be in conflict periodically.

How you live out your life roles will be influenced by a number of other key concepts which we will examine briefly.

Work

By this we do not mean simply "paid employment". Work refers to activities that can provide us with:

● a sense of purpose and direction

● a structure for living, be it regular or irregular

● a personal sense of identity and self-respect

● companions and friends

● a view of how others see and feel about us

In addition, work can provide us with money if someone wants to buy what we can do. It does not automatically provide us with money. Only paid work does that, which is why we distinguish between work and jobs. (see page 27).

We will work in the process of planning and implementing any of our life roles. We may be paid for some of that work.

Job

This is a particular position of employment one holds at any one time.

Play

This refers to activities enjoyed just for their own sake.

Income

That which is received from paid work, investments, or government social services.

Career

This is the pattern of jobs that you have had, have or hope to have. Everyone has a 'career' in this sense even when it is punctuated by periods out of paid employment, by retraining or learning, or whether a job varies from 40 hours a week to 1 hour a week.

Leisure

The time at your discretion after any paid work or day to day maintenance activities have been done is leisure time. It can include both unpaid work and play.

14

Are There Any Risks In Building Rainbows?

> *"I will get dissatisfied. If I stay as I am then I will be all right."*

No-one should be *made* to review their lives. Rainbows cannot be forced!

Our experience with adults suggests that most people benefit from occasional reviews. The parallel is visiting a GP. Many of us consult our GPs only when we are ill. We would be better advised to have periodic check-ups. As a consequence we might get ill less often.

There is no doubt that coming face-to-face with the full reality of one's dissatisfactions can be a very unsettling and sometimes painful experience. As with our bodies, however, we can only feel pain if something is wrong and needs attention. Pain is often a prerequisite to healing and growth.

"Frustration is the mother of risk"
Gail Sheehy,[3]

We will sometimes have to experience the frustration before we can be motivated to want to change.

We may be happy with things as they are, but our situation may change dramatically and automatically create a problem for us. Social and technological developments may not allow us to stand still.

Remember, that you usually need storms to bring rainbows!

> *"I might want to make dramatic changes and that could create problems for others."*

We have found all too often that people can use the anticipated fears and objections of others to mask their own anxieties and concerns. Many times we have heard statements like: "I could never do that of course, my spouse/family would never go along with it."

Our first reaction to this concern, therefore, would be to check it out to see if it was a real concern, or whose concern it really was.

We use a story to illustrate the dangers of being non-assertive about one's own needs and not checking out with others.

For one of us (and we are not saying which one!) our in-laws arrived to spend the weekend.

My wife and I were not quite sure what to do with them, yet we felt that we should make an effort to do something. We normally looked to our weekends for recuperation and our idea of a good time is to do nothing — lie in bed and get up naturally, do exactly what we feel like doing, rarely to go out, and enjoy being at home — a luxury for us. However, though neither of us wanted to do anything we thought we should offer to take them out — at least on the Sunday. We asked them if they wished to go touring the Yorkshire Dales. They said they would, so we all set off. I was doing my best to be cheery wishing all the time that I was at home reading the Sunday papers. My wife was doing her best trying to keep me happy and give her parents a good time, consequently succeeding only in giving herself a headache. We took them to a favourite pub for lunch — which didn't do lunch on Sundays! We drove them around the Dales in a force-eight gale punctuated by occasional thunderstorms. The final straw was a puncture that I had to repair in the rain.

Six hours later when we got home, I could contain myself no longer.

"Well, I think in the future we'll stick to our usual Sunday routine!"

"What's that?" they asked. So I told them.

"That sounds wonderful. We're exhausted after the week we've had. We would have loved a quiet time with our feet up."

"Why didn't you say anything?" I said through tight lips.

"You both seemed so determined to go out we didn't like to disappoint you. We thought that this was probably how you both liked to spend your Sundays!"

How often we make assumptions
about the needs of others and
remain non-assertive about our own.

But what if our desires really do clash with
those people close to us?

Our answer to that would be that probably all
that this process has done has brought
forward in time something that would have
happened in any case. Where differences
exist it is usually better to bring them out into
the open where they can be examined,
negotiations take place, bargaining if needs
be, or at least an open discussion about the
differences.

> *"What does it say about me if I keep changing
> my mind about what I want?"*

It says, simply, that you are normal. You are
more rather than less likely to change with the
years.

Between young adulthood and middle-age (a
20 year period) people have been shown to
change 52% of their interests, 55% of their
vocational interests, 69% of their self-rated
personality characteristics and 92% of their
answers to questions about their attitudes.
The research which demonstrated this was
carried out by Kelly[7] in 1955. What would the
equivalent research show today with the more
dramatic rate of social change?

All too often we decide on goals for ourselves
in our teens or twenties, and then we age and
develop, yet still work towards goals that may
not be appropriate to the different people that
we have become.

*"All my life, or at least it seemed that way, I
had wanted to be the managing director of
———————. It is only now that I realise
that the real reason I wanted that in my
twenties was that then I couldn't think of any
other criteria of real success. It's taken me
until now to realise that I have been
successful in so many ways – in my work,
with the family life I have created, in my circle
of friends. And you know, if I really look at the
way the M.D. lives, I wouldn't want that life-
style. Yet, I've struggled for years to get
somewhere I now know I don't want to get to
and I've been giving myself a bad time for not
getting there!"*

(A Marketing Manager of a
large company, aged 46)

We were also very impressed with some advertising copy we
came across in the USA selling a particular make of car, and
thought it was so relevant to career and life management:

"HAVING ARRIVED DOESN'T MEAN MUCH IF
YOU'RE BORED GETTING THERE"

"Each path is only one of a million paths.
Therefore, you must always keep in mind that
a path is only a path. If you feel that you must
not follow it, you need not stay with it under
any circumstances. Any path is only a path.
There is no affront to yourself or others in
dropping it if that is what your heart tells you
to do."

Carlos Castenada

> *"I can have all the 'fantasies' I like, but I am
> still limited by what's available and what I will
> be allowed to do."*

There is no denying that there are very real
constraints operating on us no matter how
self-empowered we are. Single-handedly we
cannot change the economy, prevent political
disasters, give ourselves superior talents that
we do not possess, or turn back our biological
time-clocks. But we find that people
consistently over-estimate the factors over
which they can have no influence and under-
estimate those that they can influence.

We sometimes use a poster on workshops which says:

"YOU CAN EITHER HAVE WHAT YOU WANT OR
HAVE THE EXCUSE FOR NOT HAVING IT"

That, as a statement of fact, is somewhat
dubious – but it makes the point.

Rainbows begin in the clouds and that is where
we need to begin also. Life's constraints are all
too obvious and can prevent us from
exercising our imaginations. The view from the
clouds can be very different from the limited
horizons we can see from the ground. Having
seen it we may choose to return to earth in a
different place.

Similarly, there is often a distinction between
what one could do and what we think society
tells us that we should do. Sometimes we fail
to begin to build rainbows because we are the
'wrong' age, the 'wrong' sex, or lack
'qualifications'.

Age stereotyping is very real and happens all
the time. On page 74 you can explore your own

attitudes to ageing and discover how far you yourself contribute to "ageism". Much age stereotyping is reflected in social attitudes, rarely based on facts. Some, sadly, are reflected by real constraints placed upon people concerning when they may enter a particular occupation. Until very recently it was impossible to apply for civil service jobs unless you were under 28. That limit has now been raised to 45, depending on the grade, but in practice it is still rare for anyone to be recruited over 24. The demographic changes in the 1990's with fewer young people available are forcing employers to look again at attracting and developing older people.

Sex-role expectations undoubtedly are a very real barrier to rainbow-building. The work of the Equal Opportunities Commission and subsequent legislation have all helped to widen horizons for both sexes, but the current research findings are depressingly predictable. Teachers encourage boys more in their learning and career aspirations[8], parents still behave differently to the sexes even before birth. Employers are still blinkered with the assumptions of yesteryear.

We all have a vital role in working for a future in which there are not two sets of rainbows – one with a pink hue and another with a blue one!

> *"I don't like the idea of planning for the future. It takes away all the spontaneity from life."*

Career and life management is not dedicated to forcing people to plan their lives away. It is dedicated to helping people gain more control over what happens to them. Neither of the present authors likes to plan more than 6-12 months ahead. That is our personal preference, but we have learned that about ourselves by discovering more about who we are and what we want from life.

Other people like to create 5 year, 10 year or lifelong plans. There is no right or wrong way. Those of us with short term inclinations could do well to force ourselves occasionally to look long term, and the lifelong planners need to remind themselves that any long term plan needs periodic reviewing.

The seeming paradox of career and life management is that the more attention we give to reviewing our needs, determining our priorities, setting objectives, the more likely

we are to provide ourselves with gift vouchers of time to exchange for anything we, spontaneously, might choose to do.

> *"What happens if I try to make changes and I don't get what I want? Aren't I worse off than before I started?"*

We believe that the straight answer has to be 'NO'. Unless we risk change we will never gain access to its fruits.

"Risk is the tariff for leaving the Land of Predictable Misery."
Howard Figler

Rainbow building will rarely leave us worse off even if it doesn't turn out as we would have wished. The process of career and life management will have involved us in learning a great deal about ourselves and also in developing the 7 crucial rainbow-building skills which we can use on other occasions.

Perhaps the final rejoinder will always remain: "If you don't try it you'll never know just what you can build for yourself."

Each of us will have opportunities sometimes. The better equipped we are with career and life management skills the greater the chance of being able to capitalise on those opportunities. Carlos Castenada talks of the importance of recognising our "cubic centimetres of chance" – the skill of recognising chances when they occur and having the courage to pursue them.

"All of us, whether or not we are warriors, have a cubic centimetre of chance that pops up in front of our eyes from time to time. The difference between the average man and the warrior is that the warrior is aware of this, and one of his tasks is to be alert and deliberately waiting so that when his cubic centimetre pops up he has the speed, the prowess to pick it up."

Carlos Castenada

Remember, it is only the mediocre who are always at their best!

The Exercises

The book contains exercises designed to help you collect data to answer the 6 key questions for career and life management. These exercises are there to help you and should not represent an obstacle race. If any particular exercise does not seem relevant to you, don't do it.

Each exercise is also designed to help you develop one of the key 7 career and life management skills. The particular skill or skills will be indicated at the beginning of an exercise. The exercises which are asterisked* are all ones we believe to be crucial to building your own rainbows. We have additional exercises that we also feel could be illuminating, but if time is short you might skip or leave these until another time.

You may choose not to complete some of the optional exercises because they are not relevant to you or where you are now. Beware, however, that you may not feel like completing some of them because you may be wary of what reflections of yourself will be revealed to you. Ask yourself then if that is sufficient reason for not doing the work.

Some space is provided for writing in your answers.

Route Maps

Each of the 6 career and life management questions will be introduced by a ROUTE MAP that will be your guide to where answering the question will take you. The map will outline the exercises contained along the route and will summarise their purposes.

Keep a record

Periodically in the text you will see a picture of a box file. This will tell you when you need to make notes and keep a record.

You might well wish to keep your answers in an actual card-box, but failing this, keep them in your 'Aha!' Folder (see page 19).

Occasionally, you will see a shaded card like this:

Data needed

This always refers you back to "keep a record" files you will have from having completed earlier exercises. Your journey to building your own rainbow is not simply a straight line. There will be considerable cross-referencing.

You will sometimes be referred forward into the book. This will always be to some part of Question 6: "What if it doesn't work out?" Throughout the book you will be invited to explore yourself, your past, your visions, your fears, your assumptions. Some of this can be very demanding and even painful. The information in Question 6 could be very useful long before you would naturally reach it in the book.

Here are some other features of the text for you to look out for:

Questions The book constantly offers you questions to further the self-discovery process for you. These are always contained in this speech bubble.

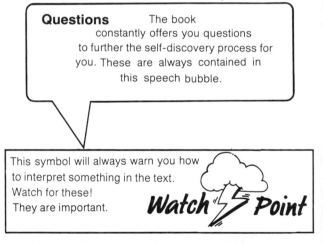

This symbol will always warn you how to interpret something in the text. Watch for these! They are important. **Watch Point**

We think it crucial to make decisions from an informed position. Throughout the book we provide what we believe to be particularly important information and statistics to stimulate your thinking. Each piece of data is heralded by this heading.

Quotations

We "fly" a number of quotations throughout the book in kites. These are intended to stimulate, summarize or simply amuse. Some will speak to you more than others.

Keeping Your Notes: Your AHA! Folder

A common finding in doing this kind of self-review is that many insights or 'Aha!' experiences can result from completing the exercises, and particularly in discussing them with a partner or group. We advise keeping a separate folder in which you put slips or sheets of paper with any insights that occur to you about yourself, your life or your career. There will be a stage towards the end of the workbook when we will ask you to empty the contents of your 'Aha!' Folder and use them as an aid to setting your objectives.

Remember, there are no right answers, only answers that are right for you.

Working with a Partner

A particular valuable strategy when faced with hours of isolated work is to link up with one other person, or even a small group of people. We would highly recommend this. Talking through these exercises not only can assist flagging motivation but other people's reactions to your efforts and thoughts are likely to be valuable and stimulating (and in turn, your reactions to their ideas could be really useful too).

A phrase we often quote is: "it takes two to see one". It can sometimes be enlightening to involve family, friends and colleagues in completing some of the assignments on you. It can also be scary! We do not recommend your choosing to work with someone who could feel threatened by what you are doing, or who might put you down or otherwise inhibit you.

Perhaps you could link up with some fellow "rainbow builders" who also contract to work with the book themselves.

A clear contract is essential.

- when are you going to meet?
- how often and for how long?
- what work will you have to complete for each session?
- how will you operate as a pair or a group?

"Seen with new eyes, our lives can be transformed from accidents into adventures"

Marilyn Ferguson

Checking your Progress

Throughout the book there will be opportunities to pause, review your progress and see what is to come next. At the end of each of the 6 cloud questions there is a summary chart which will help you to collect together all your data for that question.

Timing

We have deliberately not suggested times for the exercises. We have found that people need to spend different amounts of time for the same exercises. We do suggest that you ensure that you have sufficient time to finish a "block" on your route map. The end of a block is always signified by a PROGRESS CHECK.

Building A Contract With This Book

By now some goals, however hazy, might be forming in your head. Perhaps you are thinking –. "I'll give it another few pages to see if this is the kind of thing I am interested in," or "It really might be useful to carry out some of the exercises they are saying will follow". We invite you, therefore, to think carefully at this stage about just what you might want from a book on career and life management. To do this we want to introduce you to the concept of "contracting" – in itself a vital career and life management skill.

'Contracts' need not only be formal, written documents. There can be psychological contracts too, which at some stage can be written down but not necessarily. Contracting is a process of clarifying objectives and making agreements. I can contract with a friend to go on holiday, with a spouse to apportion out household tasks, with a doctor to make some lifestyle changes. A contract usually involves two parties and requires us to be razor-specific about what we want, what we are prepared to do and what we expect from the other party.

The advantage of conscious contracting, as opposed to half-formed or unexpressed expectations is that it demands clarity

of objectives, and as the poster says "if you don't know where you're going, you'll probably end up somewhere else". It also minimises the possibilities of misunderstanding. We often experience and live with more problems than we need to because we do not 'contract' clearly with people, organisations, and – yes – with ourselves too!

It *is* possible to talk of making a contract with yourself, and that is exactly what we invite you to do if you are ready to commit yourself to career and life management right now. Contracting is, for some people, really quite difficult but we believe it is crucial. We are offering you a contract on page 20. We have signed it. We invite you to complete this contract with us. You will be offered a chance to review it midway through the book. So, before reading any further, sit back, get comfortable, rid your mind of distractions and ask yourself the questions on the next page.

CONTRACT

BETWEEN MYSELF AND THIS WORK BOOK

1.

What will this book offer me?

This is <u>our</u> contribution to your contract. We will be inviting you to complete
a number of exercises, and to answer some questions. We will be taking you on a
carefully thought-out sequence of steps designed to help you ask and answer the 6 key
questions for career and life management outlined earlier. We estimate
a time commitment of approximately 48 hours to read the book and complete the
assignments. This will increase if you work with a partner or a group of people.

2.

What do I really want to get from reading this book? Be as specific as possible.

3.

What can I personally do to make sure that I get what I want?

4.

Based on past experience what can I do to avoid sabotaging myself,
thereby not getting what I want? What can I do to prevent this?

5.

How do I normally feel and behave if my expectations are not being met? How helpful
is this for me? What can I do to ensure my expectations will be met?

Signed by the reader   Signed on behalf of this book

Barrie Hopson   Mike Scally

Question 1
WHO AM I?

We begin with YOU as you are now. But how accurate a representation is any snapshot – an arbitrary moment of frozen time? You need to know something of your history and get a perspective on your future. YOU are the living repository of your own history, shaped by it, influenced through it and part-creator of it. To begin to focus on the context of one's life to date – the events, the experiences, the peaks, the troughs, stresses sought and imposed, decisions made, decisions made for us, and the key people who populate our biographies.

What you have done, been and learned so far will be your launching pad for the future.

ROUTE MAP for "Who am I?"

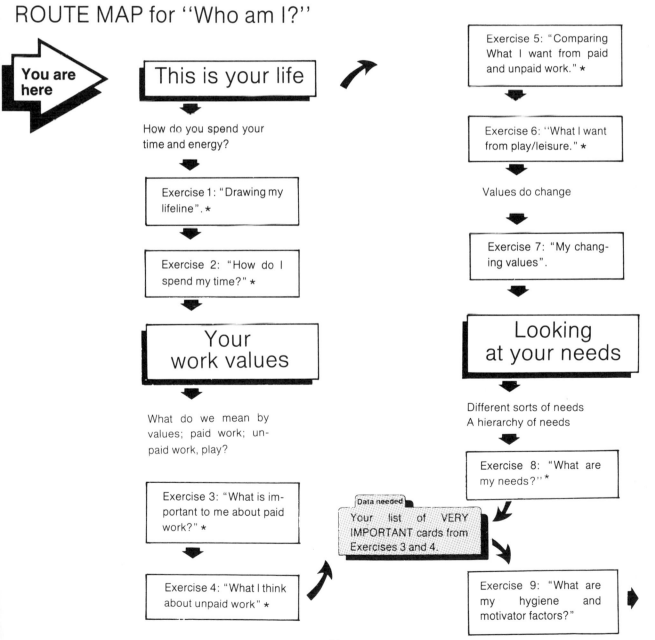

You are here

This is your life

How do you spend your time and energy?

Exercise 1: "Drawing my lifeline". ★

Exercise 2: "How do I spend my time?" ★

Your work values

What do we mean by values; paid work; unpaid work, play?

Exercise 3: "What is important to me about paid work?" ★

Exercise 4: "What I think about unpaid work" ★

Data needed
Your list of VERY IMPORTANT cards from Exercises 3 and 4.

Exercise 5: "Comparing What I want from paid and unpaid work." ★

Exercise 6: "What I want from play/leisure." ★

Values do change

Exercise 7: "My changing values".

Looking at your needs

Different sorts of needs
A hierarchy of needs

Exercise 8: "What are my needs?" ★

Exercise 9: "What are my hygiene and motivator factors?"

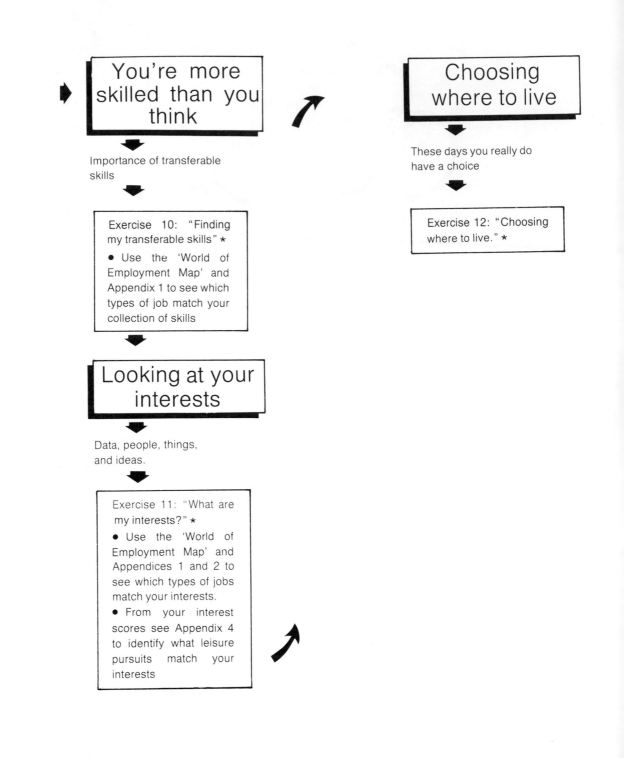

You're more skilled than you think

Importance of transferable skills

Exercise 10: "Finding my transferable skills" ★

• Use the 'World of Employment Map' and Appendix 1 to see which types of job match your collection of skills

Looking at your interests

Data, people, things, and ideas.

Exercise 11: "What are my interests?" ★

• Use the 'World of Employment Map' and Appendices 1 and 2 to see which types of jobs match your interests.

• From your interest scores see Appendix 4 to identify what leisure pursuits match your interests

Choosing where to live

These days you really do have a choice

Exercise 12: "Choosing where to live." ★

This Is Your Life

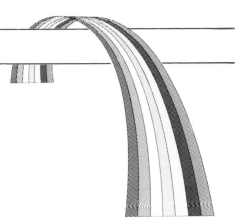

Exercise 1: Drawing my lifeline.*

RAINBOW BUILDING SKILL: Learning from experience

- Take a very large sheet of paper and draw a line which represents your life. This might be a straight line, or one with peaks and troughs – we have even seen a spiral! It's shape is to be determined by you only.

- Indicate on the line where you are NOW with a large X.

- Mark in the key events or happenings in your life on the line, starting with events as early as you can remember and proceed to the present.

- Leave plenty of space between the years. You will find that one memory triggers off another, so be prepared to move back and forth along the line as the memories flow back to you.

- Now look back at each event and ask yourself the following questions, putting the appropriate symbol or symbols after each one. For some events none of the symbols might apply.

Was this a Peak Experience?   △

Was this a Trough Experience?   ∪

Was there Important Learning for me in this   !

How Stressful was it? Rate this on the scale: S = somewhat stressful, SS = stressful, SSS = very stressful

Did I take a Risk?   R

Did I Choose to do this?   √

Or did I have No choice?   X

Take as much time as you need to do this – THIS IS YOUR LIFE!

After you have completed this, look at the following list of questions. They may not all be appropriate to you. Select those that are relevant to you or that trigger off reactions in you.

Write down your answers and add any thoughts, ideas or objectives which occur to you, and make a note of them in your AHA! FOLDER.

> What does this account of my life so far say about me and how I have lived my life?
>
> Does anything surprise me?
>
> What are the most important elements in my peak experiences?

This will help you to identify those things that are really crucial to you in life.

> What elements characterise the trough or low points in my life?
>
> What have I learned (a) from my peak experiences (b) from my low points?

Do I take risks? Do they turn out mostly positively or negatively for me?

Does my life divide into themes? What unfinished themes are there? Are there any changes in my life pattern with age?

Keep a record
- My life line
- Notes about my life so far

Exercise 2: How do I spend my time?*

RAINBOW BUILDING SKILL: Knowing yourself

What you have done so far is to step back and take a long look at your life overall as you have lived it up to *now*. The next step is to examine in greater detail just how you are investing your time right now.

It consistently surprises us that we so often encounter people who spend large periods of time analysing returns and payoffs for their investments, working out the 'best buy' for a refrigerator, cassette tape or brand of marmalade, and yet do not transfer their considerable analytical skills to their own lives.

- What returns am I getting for the time and energy I am expending

- What parts of my life are 'best buys'?

- How am I *actually* filling the hours of each day?

What we have discovered is that our memories of how we spend our time are notoriously unreliable. Weight control specialists have known for some time that asking people what they have eaten is very inaccurate. The only accurate way is to ask them to record each day what they do eat.

We invite you to do the same with your use of time.

- Over one week keep a record of your activities. Begin on any day you like, but it will be most useful if you can choose a fairly typical week and 'log it'.

- It is best done by doing the recording at the end of each day or even periodically through the day. We provide one chart below which we have found useful, but if this breakdown – into 2 hour slots – does not fit for you, do create your own. You will need a large sheet of paper.

- This is a crucial piece of data collection. You will be asked to refer back to it for Question 3 "How satisfied am I with who and where I am?"

- This log will take you a week to complete, but you can continue with the other exercises, returning to this exercise when you have completed the log.

When your record is complete, answer the following questions:

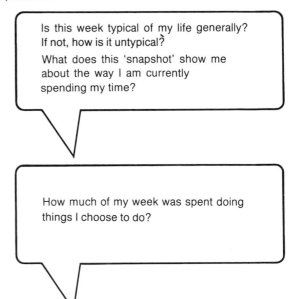

Is this week typical of my life generally? If not, how is it untypical?

What does this 'snapshot' show me about the way I am currently spending my time?

How much of my week was spent doing things I choose to do?

TIME INVESTMENT RECORD

	am 12-2	2-4	4-6	6-8	8-10	10-12	pm 12-2	2-4	4-6	6-8	8-10	10-12
MONDAY												
TUESDAY												
WEDNESDAY												
THURSDAY												
FRIDAY												
SATURDAY												
SUNDAY												

Fill in the bar chart below to indicate what percentage of time is
spent in your different roles. (Some of your life roles will overlap so that your totals will probably be well over 100%).

LIFE ROLE	PERCENTAGE OF TIME SPENT						
	10%	20%	30%	40%	50%	60%	70-100%
CHILD							
EMPLOYEE							
SPOUSE							
PARENT							
CITIZEN							
CONSUMER							
FRIEND							
LEISURE-USER							
STUDENT/LEARNER							
HOME-MAKER							
OTHER							
OTHER							

Each of us is potentially the difference in the world.
Marilyn Ferguson,
The Aquarian Conspiracy

Keep a record

- My time investment record
- Notes about the way I use time

The way to succeed is to double your failure rate.
Thomas J. Watson, founder of IBM.

WHO AM I?

What have you learned about how you have been living your life until now?

....
....
....
....
....
....
....
....
....
....
....
....
....

You have now reviewed your life overall and have examined how you spend your time right now.

It is now time to collect data about key aspects of yourself. The next section will provide you with information about:

Your VALUES

Your INTERESTS

Your SKILLS

Where you wish to LIVE AND WORK

What STAGE OF LIFE you are at now

What kind of CAREER PATTERN you want to have

Your Work Values

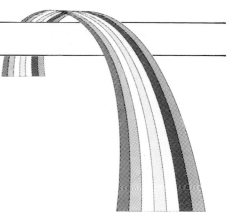

Whenever you ask yourself questions like:

"Where do I want to live and work?"

"How do I like to spend my time?"

"What kind of people do I choose to have around me?"

"How important to me is money, status, autonomy, success, security, creativity, power, helping others, spontaneity, risk taking?"

you are asking questions about your values. Being able to answer questions like these, therefore, clearly plays a key role in career and life management. The more you are able to live out your values the more rewarding your lives will be.

In this section we will be focussing on what you value in WORK (paid and unpaid), and PLAY.

Work Values

On page 28 we distinguish between PAID work and UNPAID work, claiming that we will work in the process of planning and implementing any of our life roles — child, homemaker, consumer, citizen, student, employee, spouse, parent, leisure-user, friend, etc.

What is work?

- It is an activity.

- It can provide us with a sense of purpose and direction.

- It can provide a structure for living, although that might be regular or irregular.

- It can provide a personal sense of identity and self-respect.

- It can provide us with companions and friends

- It can influence how other people see and feel about us.

- It can, in addition, provide us with money if someone wants to buy what we can do.

We distinguish clearly between work and jobs. Real work is available for all of us, even if jobs are not. We must separate out the issue of income from that of work. This is not to say that income is not important. It is of crucial importance to us all, and is a political issue demanding decisions from our society on how wealth should be distributed. Everyone needs work, everyone needs income, but not everyone can get a job, in the traditional sense, nor wants one.

You may well ask:

"What is wrong with equating work with a job?"

It is not so much that it is 'wrong', but that the consequences of the link are increasingly misleading and a source of distress for many people.

— The person who is a full-time homemaker certainly works, but if those activities are not considered as work, there is little status that attaches to it and the person can be discouraged from finding value in the work.

— People who choose to be full-time parents, whilst possibly gaining a little more social status, are often still regarded and too often regard themselves as unproductive.

— People who do not have a job at all are generally thought to be unproductive and can be the focus of considerable social criticism. This is why unemployment is a social stigma still today, and why the unemployed are viewed by the employed with a mixture of concern and suspicion.

— People who choose to be employed for less than the national average, i.e. for half-time or one-third time, or even four-fifths time, are sometimes viewed as lacking commitment and shirking their responsibilities.

"There is likely to be a shortage of employment as we have traditionally known it in the forseeable future. But while there may be a shortage of jobs there will never be a shortage of work."

What is taken as 'normal employment' is, of course, always historically limited to its era. Normal employment in the mid-nineteenth century was a six-day week, ten hours a day, with a week of public holidays only to look forward to.

The particular problem that we are experiencing today reflects the age old tradition of equating 'work' with 'labour', in particular, manual labour, by definition hard, often dirty and to many consequently demeaning. This was then linked to a peculiarly modern idea deriving from the Industrial Era. The industrial revolution demanded that vast numbers of people should leave their homes to operate machines and to service the vast bureaucracies necessary to manage the production and distribution of the new wealth. The methods of production were voracious for human labour. For many years men, women and even children were 'employed'. (The concept of employment, interestingly, cannot be found in references before 1830). It became normal for people, and increasingly just men, to have jobs in the new system, so much so, that jobs came to be synonymous with work. In the Industrial Era the equation was born:

$$WORK = JOB$$

We launched a campaign from Lifeskills Associates in 1983 to break this equation, and we symbolized the campaign with the logo

$$WORK \neq JOB$$

Work does not equal a job. It is far broader than that.

Today, a job is typically seen as paid work involving a five-day week, seven to eight hours a day, with four weeks annual holi-day. By the year AD 2000 it is likely to have been reduced to an average of thirty hours a week, up to eight weeks annual holi-day and a bevy of employment alternatives incorporating job-sharing, flexitime, a compressed working week, flexiplace, in-dustrial sabbaticals, multi-job holding, and the gradual disap-pearance of the concept of 'part-time' employment. It is only possible to have 'part-time' employment if there is a consensus on what 'full-time' is. Already one in five employees in the UK works part-time and the proportion is increasing.

We can eliminate some of the confusion by looking at the different kinds of emphasis given to work throughout history. These range from activities that we like doing to those that we dislike doing. Then there is work we are paid for and that for which we receive no direct financial reward. This is shown in the following chart.

TYPES OF WORK

	LIKED	DISLIKED
PAID	A job in which the work is intrinsically rewarding. You might even do this for little or no pay.	A job involving work which you would not choose to do unless you needed the money.
UNPAID	An activity you enjoy or feel is useful. You do it for no other reason.	Activities you do not enjoy but are obliged to do by force or con-tractual agreement.

Types of work

We have expounded at length about the concept of WORK because we see it as being a concept central to this book for WORK is central to each of us.

An example may help to explain why definitions of work can vary so greatly. Let us examine the activity of *gardening* as it might appear to different people at different times.

Liked/paid work:

This person loves gardening for its own sake. It is a source of delight to him that he actually gets paid for it also. It is his major source of income.

Disliked/paid work:

This person does not especially like gardening. If he did not have to earn money he would not choose to do it. He does it because there are no other jobs, or because he likes this better than the other jobs available to him.

Liked/unpaid work:

This person also loves gardening but either cannot get paid for doing it or would not choose to do it as his major source of income for a variety of reasons – he likes doing other things more, or it does not pay as much as he wants to earn. This activity has traditionally been labelled a *leisure pursuit* or a *hobby*.

Disliked/unpaid work:

This person does not enjoy gardening. He has an arrangement with his wife, however, that he will do the gardening if she will do the housework as both agree that it needs to be done.

The scenario gets even more complicated as the nature of the work can change because the situation changes or because the person changes. For example, the disliked/unpaid work of gardening may only feel like that when you don't really have the time, the weather is disgusting or you feel unwell. Similarly, as a result of having to garden, what began as a chore can sometimes be transformed into a pleasure as you discover new facets of your skills and personality.

As an illustration of how the concepts of work and employment are changing, we reproduce for you two scenario's, one of which encapsulates the views of 40 years ago and the other demonstrates how views about work and jobs are changing so rapidly.

"We are living at at time when history is holding its breath, and the present is detaching itself from its moorings to sail across the boundless ocean".

Arthur C Clarke

Which of the two career counselling sessions that follow were closest to your experience? (If you did not yourself receive any vocational guidance you will almost certainly still have picked up some of the messages conveyed in these scenarios).

Scenario: Vocational Guidance in 1956

In the youth employment officer's (Y.E.O.) office

Y.E.O.   "Well, John, you're 17 now and it's time for you to choose the career in which you would like to spend the rest of your life."

JOHN   "What should I be looking for?"

Y.E.O.   "That depends upon your own interests and abilities, and qualifications, but generally I would advise that you looked for a job that has good training, good promotion prospects and where you can find total satisfaction for the whole of your working life if you choose."

JOHN   "What if I change my mind about what I want when I've been in it for a while?"

Y.E.O.   "Don't change your mind too often. Employers don't like it. It doesn't look good on your CV. But, if you do, you have a good education behind you, good examination results — these will keep you in good stead for any move you might wish to make in later life."

JOHN   "I'm thinking that a career in marketing might be for me. I enjoy travel and would be interested in a job that enabled me to travel abroad and maybe live abroad for a while."

Y.E.O.   "That's fine, but what will you do when you get married?"

JOHN   "My wife would come with me. There might be an office job she could do in the company. Of course, if we had any children she will be fully occupied anyway."

Y.E.O.   "Quite."

JOHN   "What kind of holidays could I expect?"

Y.E.O.   "Many jobs at your level now offer at least two and sometimes three weeks holiday a year. You can expect to work a basic 44 hour week, but on a salary you will be expected to work longer than that for no extra pay."

JOHN   "How secure is a job in marketing?"

Y.E.O.   "It has more risks attached to it than some jobs, but the economy is booming. We are not likely to see anything like the 1930's depression again. All political parties are totally committed to full employment and there are some desperate labour shortages. You'll never be short of a job."

JOHN   "Of course, I do have other interests — my tennis, mountaineering, and I play the guitar. I will want to leave time for them."

Y.E.O.   "So you should, but be careful. Your job must come first. Your company will be investing a great deal of money in your training and will expect some loyalty and commitment in return. Do well by them and you will be well looked after for life."

JOHN   "Where can I learn about marketing?"

Y.E.O.   "We have booklets which give you all the information you need on the vast range of work that's available."

JOHN   "Thank you. My father finds all this difficult to understand. He says I shouldn't be so choosy and just to be grateful that I've got a job."

Y.E.O.   "That's understandable if you think what he went through in the 30's. But today the world is your oyster."

Scenario: Life and Career Management in 1996

In the career counsellor's office

COUNSELLOR   "Well, John, I know that you will have been doing a lot of thinking in your school about yourself and your future. What is important to you? How do you want to live your life?"

JOHN   "I enjoy learning very much and whatever I do I would want it to be something where I am constantly learning about new things."

COUNSELLOR   "That will almost be inevitable whatever you decide to do. Do you know, for example, that the Electricians Union in the USA has 60 people solely rewriting textbooks because about 10% of the technical knowledge in the industry becomes obsolete each year. Also, it has been calculated that at the rate at which information is accumulating now there is four times the amount of information available than was the case when you started school. By the time you are 50 it is likely to be over 30 times greater and more than 90% of everything known will have been discovered during your lifetime!"

JOHN   "So I am always going to be learning new things?"

COUNSELLOR   "You will have to, whether it's in relation to your paid work or your unpaid work."

JOHN   "What are my chances of finding work?"

COUNSELLOR   "Excellent! There is never a shortage of work, even if there is a shortage of jobs. But in the foreseeable future young people will be in high demand as there are fewer of you. Mind you, you may have to change your views about a job as being something you work in for 40 hours a week for 48 weeks a year for 48 years of your life."

JOHN   "My father finds all this difficult to understand. He thinks that unless I have a job like he used to have – that I'll never amount to anything."

COUNSELLOR   "You have to remember that life was like that when he was your age. Then you could get a job for life. Now you can expect 3 or 4 occupational changes in your lifetime, 3 or 4 job changes every 10 years. There will be some periods of your life with no job at all, and others where you will be employed but for considerably fewer hours than your father was used to.

Do you know that by the year 2000 an expert has calculated that 75% of the population are likely to be in jobs that do not yet exist? 25% of all jobs are now part-time. 10% of employees are self-employed. By the end of the century possibly 40–50% of people will be working from their homes. The figure is already 25%. Our views about jobs and work are having to change dramatically."

JOHN   "So you're saying that I will need to find what kinds of work I want to do, but that I will only get paid for some of it?"

COUNSELLOR   "That's right. You can find interesting work at home, in your leisure time, doing things in the community and by learning new things at college, through home study, TV courses, etc."

JOHN   "But my father says I need a job with prospects, a job for life."

COUNSELLOR   "You're very unlikely to get one. Even if you do, what he understood by a 'job for life' would be very different. Then it meant until you retired at 65. As you know, the majority of large organisations now ease people out at around 50 to begin new careers or to retire or to be partly retired."

JOHN   "I'd like a job where I could travel and maybe live abroad, like in marketing."

COUNSELLOR   "What would happen when you got married?"

JOHN   "Well, we would have to talk it through – see whose career was most important at that time. My career might have to wait it's turn. But I want my wife to have a career, because with two incomes we will both be freer to do what we want if either of us get dissatisfied."

COUNSELLOR   "I think you would do well to get a variety of experience. Employers are sometimes suspicious of people who never move. It looks as though they are not taking any responsibility for their own careers."

JOHN   "But I think employers should look after their staffs."

COUNSELLOR   "They used to – and demanded loyalty in return. They can't expect that any more. They lost that when they made millions redundant in the late 70's and early 80's. These days you need to manage your own career, and they expect that. Tell me, what else are you interested in?"

JOHN	"I enjoy programming my computer – in fact I've got quite a reputation as a debugger and chaser of 'glitches'. I play electric guitar and have started to compose some music on my computer. I play football, enjoy cooking – especially Chinese, and help my mother out on Saturday's at a market stall, selling computer games and equipment for home micro's."
COUNSELLOR	"If you're not successful in getting in to marketing there would appear to be a number of other income producing possibilities, plus, you certainly seem to have a full life."
JOHN	"I'm never bored. In fact there never seems to be enough time. But how do I find out more about marketing?"
COUNSELLOR	"I'll book you some time at our computer terminal. It will help you to discover your skills, interests and identify your key values. It will then suggest a number of options. You can call up some information there and then and take a printout home with you. I can also lend you some videos to show at home on life in marketing or whatever other occupations you would like to explore. The computer will talk to you at first in terms of grouped jobs rather than specific jobs, and will relate your profile to them. You are almost certainly equipped for a far wider range of jobs or groups of jobs than you will be aware of right now."

The next thirty years are likely to see an even more rapid rate of change which will contain its own set of unpredictables. Some of the future we can predict, the problem is that we cannot be certain of which bits. What we can be certain about is that we will all have to be more flexible and adaptable than at any other time in our history. To equip ourselves for unknown scenarios we will need the broad range of personal competencies that we call "Lifeskills" – knowing not just how to read and write, but how to find and use information, how to make, keep and end relationships, how to manage change, how to be assertive, how to learn, how to give and receive feedback, how to manage stress, how to make decisions and solve problems, how to manage time, how to communicate, manage conflict, develop self-confidence, and to discover what we want to do with our lives.

Paul Valery remarked that the trouble with our time is that the future is not what it used to be!

RAINBOW BUILDING SKILLS: Knowing yourself
Making decisions

On the four separate sheets marked 'MY VALUES CARDS' on pages 33 to 39 you will find cards to cut out which include 5 with the following headings:

VERY IMPORTANT
IMPORTANT
QUITE IMPORTANT
OF SOME IMPORTANCE
NOT IMPORTANT

- Cut out the pages indicated and then cut up the cards so that you have a pack of 35 Work Values cards and 5 heading cards.

- Place the 5 heading cards in front of you as indicated:

VERY IMPORTANT	IMPORTANT	QUITE IMPORTANT	OF SOME IMPORTANCE	NOT IMPORTANT

Look at each of the 35 work values cards and ask yourself the question:

"How important is this aspect of work to me when I am considering PAID WORK?"

- After sorting the cards into 5 columns, make certain that there are no more than 7 or 8 in the VERY IMPORTANT pile. If there are, we would suggest that you are not discriminating finely enough between the things that are important to you and we would encourage you to discriminate further.

- If there are some important values for you not represented on the cards create your own extra cards and add them to the sorting task.

- Rank-order your VERY IMPORTANT cards from the most to the least important.

- Look at MY PAID WORK VALUES chart on page 41 and write in your rank-ordered VERY IMPORTANT work values in the left hand column.

- Write in your NOT IMPORTANT cards in the space provided.

You now have a tool you can use to analyse the suitability of any paid work prospect including your present job if you have one. You will move on in a moment to analyse your UNPAID WORK VALUES.

"By working faithfully 8 hours a day you may eventually get to be a boss and work 12 hours".

Anon

OF SOME IMPORTANCE	NOT IMPORTANT

QUITE IMPORTANT	VERY IMPORTANT

IMPORTANT	**PLACE OF WORK** It is important that you work in the right part of the country for you.

PEACE You prefer to have few pressures or uncomfortable demands.	**VARIETY** You enjoy having lots of different things to do.

COMPETITION You enjoy competing against other people or groups.	**INDEPENDENCE** You like being able to work in the way you want, without others telling you what to do.

HAVING

BEING

TIME FREEDOM

You prefer to be able to choose your own times for doing things, not having rigid working hours.

FRIENDSHIP

You would or do like close friendships with people at work.

FAST PACE

You enjoy working rapidly at a high pace.

STATUS

You enjoy being in a position which leads other people to respect you.

MAKING DECISIONS

It is important to you to have to make decisions about how things should be done, who should do it and when it should be done.

CREATIVITY

Thinking up new ideas and ways of doing things is important to you.

RISK

You like to take risks.

EXCITEMENT

It is important for you to have a lot of excitement in your work.

MONEY

Earning a large amount of money is important to you.

HELPING OTHERS

It is important to you to help other people either individually or in groups, as part of your work.

DOING

DOING

BEING

BEING

HAVING

A WELL-KNOWN ORGANISATION

You like being part of a well-known organisation.

PROMOTION

You like to work where there is a good chance of promotion.

CHALLENGE

You enjoy being 'stretched' and given new problems to work on.

ROUTINE

You like a work routine which is fairly predictable.

PRESSURE

You like working to deadlines.

COMMUNITY

You like to live in a place where you can get involved in the community.

WORK WITH OTHERS

You like to work in a team alongside others.

PHYSICAL CHALLENGE

You enjoy doing something that is physically demanding.

WORK ALONE

You like to work on your own

ARTISTIC

You enjoy work involving drawing, designing, making music, making models, etc.

DOING

HAVING   BEING

DOING

                                                    DOING

COMMUNICATION
You enjoy being able to express ideas well in writing or in speech.

RECOGNITION
You do like people to appreciate you for the work you do.

SECURITY
It is important to know your work will always be there for you.

CONTACT WITH PEOPLE
You enjoy having a lot of contact with people.

PRECISE WORK
You like working at things which involve great care and concentration.

HELP SOCIETY
You like to think that your work is producing something worthwhile for society.

SUPERVISION
You enjoy being responsible for work done by others.

PERSUADING PEOPLE
You enjoy persuading people to buy something or change their minds about something.

LEARNING
It is important for you to learn new things.

BEING EXPERT
You like being known as someone with special knowledge or skills.

DOING

DOING   HAVING

BEING

DOING   BEING

40

Looking at your present job

Ask yourself this question about each of your very important work values:

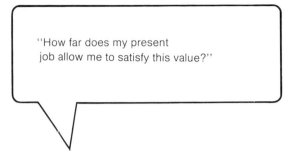

"How far does my present job allow me to satisfy this value?"

If your present job totally satisfies that value you can give it 10 points.

If that value is never satisfied in that job you award it 0 points.

Please use the full range from 0–10.

Fill in your scores in the space___on the chart.

You will see that a weighting of your answers has already been filled in for you. Simply complete the calculations. For example:

_6_ x 8 = 48

_8_ x 7 = 56

_2_ x 6 = 12 etc.

The columns for Job Alternatives are explained on the next page.

MY PAID WORK VALUES			
VERY IMPORTANT	MY PRESENT JOB	JOB ALTERNATIVE No. 1	JOB ALTERNATIVE No. 2
1.	___ x 8 –	___ x 8 =	___ x 8 =
2.	___ x 7 =	___ x 7 =	___ x 7 =
3.	___ x 6 =	___ x 6 =	___ x 6 =
4.	___ x 5 =	___ x 5 =	___ x 5 =
5.	___ x 4 =	___ x 4 =	___ x 4 =
6.	___ x 3 =	___ x 3 =	___ x 3 =
7.	___ x 2 =	___ x 2 =	___ x 2 =
8.	___ x 1 =	___ x 1 =	___ x 1 =
	TOTAL	TOTAL	TOTAL

MY NOT IMPORTANT CARDS ARE:

1. . . . .

2. . . . .

3. . . . .

4. . . . .

5. . . . .

6. . . . .

7. . . . .

8. . . . .

Tick any of these if they feature in your present job or any alternative jobs.

Add up the total for your present job. If you give 10 points for each of your 8 VERY IMPORTANT values your maximum total would be 360, although it is highly unlikely that anyone would achieve 360.

Answer the following questions for yourself:

> How much opportunity is there overall in my present job for me to find expression for those values? Do any of the values in my NOT IMPORTANT column feature in my present job? Do I find opportunities to satisfy my values in my life outside of my job?

> Can I think of any jobs other than my present one which would closely fit my key values? Are my work values different now than at other times in my life? In what way?
> Can I think of any objectives I would like to set myself as a result of this exercise?

 FACT Over half of the employed population of 6 E.E.C. countries, including the U.K., when offered a choice between pay and shorter hours chose shorter hours.

Keep a record
- My paid work values chart
- Notes about what I've discovered
- Objectives I should pursue

Looking at alternative jobs

> If you don't have a job and want one
> or
> If you have a job but are actively considering other jobs

Complete the previous exercise, but in addition, fill in your answers for as many alternative jobs as you are considering. Total up the scores for each job separately, scoring each one on how it might provide an outlet for your work values.

> How do the jobs compare in the scoring? Does this feel right? If not, why not?
>
> Do any of the jobs contain any of my NOT IMPORTANT characteristics?

> Do I need additional information before making a choice? If so, what information?
>
> Do I need to set myself any objectives?

Exercise 4: What I think about unpaid work.*

- List examples of the kinds of UNPAID WORK that you do in your life on the chart 'My Unpaid Work Values'

  For example: cleaning the house, baby-sitting, church duties, 'do-it-yourself' activities, gardening, cooking, keeping accounts for a social club, organising outings for old people, washing clothes, etc.

- Sort the cards into columns under the 5 headings by asking yourself the questions:

> What is important to me in UNPAID WORK?

- Rank order them.
- Write down your VERY IMPORTANT and NOT IMPORTANT cards.
- Use the MY UNPAID WORK VALUES CHART below – write in the activities you wish to analyse.

> How do my UNPAID WORK activities compare in the scoring? Does this feel right? If not, why not? Do any of my UNPAID WORK activities contain any of my NOT IMPORTANT values?
> Do I need to set myself any objectives?

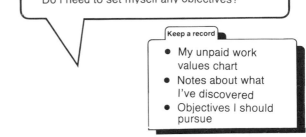

Keep a record
- My unpaid work values chart
- Notes about what I've discovered
- Objectives I should pursue

MY UNPAID WORK VALUES				
VERY IMPORTANT	ACTIVITY No. 1	ACTIVITY No. 2	ACTIVITY No. 3	ACTIVITY No. 4
1.	__ x 8 –	__ x 8 =	__ x 8 =	__ x 8 =
2.	__ x 7 =	__ x 7 =	__ x 7 =	__ x 7 =
3.	__ x 6 =	__ x 6 =	__ x 6 =	__ x 6 =
4.	__ x 5 =	__ x 5 =	__ x 5 =	__ x 5 =
5.	__ x 4 =	__ x 4 =	__ x 4 =	__ x 4 =
6.	__ x 3 =	__ x 3 =	__ x 3 =	__ x 3 =
7.	__ x 2 =	__ x 2 =	__ x 2 =	__ x 2 =
8.	__ x 1 =	__ x 1 =	__ x 1 =	__ x 1 =
	TOTAL	TOTAL	TOTAL	TOTAL

MY NOT IMPORTANT CARDS ARE:

1. . . . .

2. . . . .

3. . . . .

4. . . . .

5. . . . .

6. . . . .

7. . . . .

8. . . . .

Tick any of these if they feature in your unpaid work activities.

Exercise ·5: Comparing what I want from paid and unpaid work?*

- Complete the card sort for PAID WORK as described previously.

- Complete the card sort for UNPAID WORK.

  > Are there any differences between my VERY IMPORTANT cards for PAID and UNPAID work? What are they?
  >
  > Any differences between my NOT IMPORTANT CARDS for PAID and UNPAID WORK?

- You might like to compare your analysis with that of Bill Charlton, a participant on one of our workshops, on page 45.

on page 45.

Keep a record
- Notes about what I've discovered.

Exercise 6: What I want from play/leisure?*

- Do the card-sort again, this time asking yourself: What is important to me when I play and in my leisure activities?

- Write down the 8 most important play values in the spaces provide on the MY PLAY VALUES chart below.

- Write down your 4 favourite play or leisure activities in the spaces provided.

- Ask yourself for each activity how far your play values are being satisfied (10 = totally 0 = never)

- Write in your NOT IMPORTANT play values on the chart.

MY PLAY VALUES				
VERY IMPORTANT	PLAY No. 1	PLAY No. 2	PLAY No. 3	PLAY No. 4
1.	— x 8 =	— x 8 =	— x 8 =	— x 8 =
2.	— x 7 =	— x 7 =	— x 7 =	— x 7 =
3.	— x 6 =	— x 6 =	— x 6 =	— x 6 =
4.	— x 5 =	— x 5 =	— x 5 =	— x 5 =
5.	— x 4 =	— x 4 =	— x 4 =	— x 4 =
6.	— x 3 =	— x 3 =	— x 3 =	— x 3 =
7.	— x 2 =	— x 2 =	— x 2 =	— x 2 =
8.	— x 1 =	— x 1 =	— x 1 =	— x 1 =
	TOTAL	TOTAL	TOTAL	TOTAL

MY NOT IMPORTANT CARDS ARE:

1. . . . .

2. . . . .

3. . . . .

4. . . . .

5. . . . .

6. . . . .

7. . . . .

8. . . . .

Tick if they feature in your play activities.

Not all of the cards will fit for PLAY, e.g. promotion and place of work. Some others require translation e.g.

    Work alone = being alone
    Precise work = precise activities

Reading only the card heading, e.g. SECURITY might be more helpful than the explanations, as many of these are specifically linked to jobs.

Bill Charlton

Below we reproduce Bill's sortings of his PAID and UNPAID work values.

This is an example from one of our workshops.

PAID WORK

VERY IMPORTANT	IMPORTANT	QUITE IMPORTANT	OF SOME IMPORTANCE	NOT IMPORTANT
Independence	Artistic	Help Society	Work alone	Precise work
Creative	Well-known	Variety	Promotion	Routine
Money	organisation	Place of work	Contact with	Community
Communication	Fast Pace	Challenge	people	Physical challenge
Learning	Recognition	Risk	Pressure	Security
Friendship	Making	Status	Competition	Peaceful
Excitement	decisions	Persuading		
Time freedom	Being supervised	people		
		Helping others		
		Work with others		

UNPAID WORK

VERY IMPORTANT	IMPORTANT	QUITE IMPORTANT	OF SOME IMPORTANCE	NOT IMPORTANT
Creative	Work with	Physical	Contact	Community
Communication	others	Peaceful	with people	Routine
Artistic	Money	Work alone	Being expert	Promotion
Helping	Status	Learning	Making	Supervision
others		Help society	decisions	Fast pace
Friendship		Challenge	Persuading	Recognition
Time freedom			people	Security
Independence			Risk	Competition
Place of work			Precise work	Well-known
				organisation
				Pressure

Bill said,

"From this example it is clear that I have some values which are important to me for any work I do, whether paid or unpaid — creativity, independence, friendship, time freedom, communication. This exercise highlights just how crucial these needs are to me as a total person.

"I know what my overriding work needs are. I also know that my unpaid work needs to compensate for what I don't require as much from in my paid work, e.g. artistic, and physical challenge."

Bill Charlton

Bill's PLAY values are also reproduced.

PLAY VALUES

VERY IMPORTANT	IMPORTANT	QUITE IMPORTANT	OF SOME IMPORTANCE	NOT IMPORTANT
Independence	Variety	Friendship	Contact with	Pressure
Peaceful	Excitement	Artistic	people	Being expert
Place I am	Communication	Competition	Precise	Supervision
Creative	Routine	Security	activities	Making decisions
Physical	Recognition	Challenge	Community	Well-known
challenge	Fast pace	Being with	Help society	organisation
Being alone		others	Helping others	Persuading
Time freedom				people
Learning				Status
				Money

Bill said,

"This again underlies my central need for independence, creativity and time-freedom in all I do. It also shows how a balance between work and play is important to me, i.e. I enjoy physical challenge and competition when playing squash and other games. I also want status, money, decision-making, supervision and persuading people to have no place in my play activities."

"There is also a contrast in that my play activities must encompass both peace and physical challenge, which for me means lying in the sun reading and a hard game of squash."

"Doing the exercise made me realise just how little time I had in my life for play and that is a thought for my AHA! FOLDER."

Keep a record

- What I've discovered about my values.

VALUES DO CHANGE

Our values are a mirror image of who we are at any moment. Perhaps more dramatically we would argue that we are merely the mirror images of our values — so central are they as the 'drivers' behind our life journeys. Periodically, however, those journeys change directions — as a result of life events, growing older, and our changing views of ourselves. There is nothing unusual about that. On the contrary, there would be something more unusual if our values stayed constant.

Exercise 7: My changing values

RAINBOW BUILDING SKILL: Knowing yourself
Learning from experience

You have already sorted the values cards for what is important to you now. Do the following additional card sorts for paid work only.

- No. 1: Sort them as you might have done when you were 18 years old.

- No. 2: Sort them as if you were 30.

- No. 3: Sort them as if you were 45.

- No. 4: Sort them as if you were 65.

For some of these sortings you will be projecting into the future.

> What changes am I aware of? What do these say about me?
> What has stayed constant? What does this say about me?
> What does this say about how I see my future?

(Record this in your AHA! FOLDER. It will be useful data for QUESTION 3: WHAT CHANGES DO I WANT?)

Values and needs also change as a result of how successful we are in satisfying them!

Let us illuminate that curious statement. Abraham Maslow was an American psychologist who said that we must view human needs in a hierarchical way. By that he meant that our needs can be arranged in an order, some of which have be be satisfied before we can or want to address ourselves to a higher level of needs.

The diagram demonstrates this. From this it is clear that if your main concern is getting an income just to keep yourself alive, you are unlikely to be spending much time wondering about the cosmic importance of your place in the universe!

It also follows that at certain periods of your life you may revert to a lower level of need, for example, on being suddenly made redundant, or losing a spouse.

Again, this re-adjustment of your needs should not in itself be a cause for concern. This reaction is a normal response to events such as these. It does not mean that in some way you have regressed.

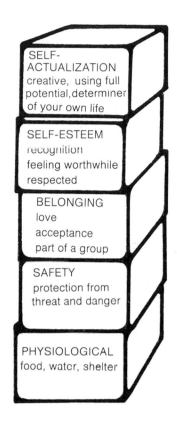

MASLOW'S LEVELS OF NEEDS

FACT The growth occupations are in health, electronics, security, banking, insurance, professional and scientific services and adult education.

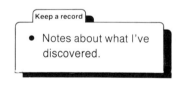

Keep a record
- Notes about what I've discovered.

"If work were a good thing the rich would have found a way of keeping it all to themselves."

Haitian proverb

47

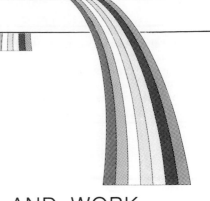

Exercise 8: What are my needs?*

RAINBOW BUILDING SKILL: Knowing yourself

Our values, simply, are an expression of our needs. This exercise will give you an opportunity to discover where you are on Maslow's levels of needs diagram. One thing you will discover is that you are unlikely to find that you are living totally at one level of need.

● On the back of some of the Work Values cards are printed the following words:

HAVING   DOING   BEING

These cards represent examples of the needs in the hierarchy. Our physiological and safety needs can be grouped together as indicating things we HAVE to have before we can focus on anything else.

Our belonging and self-esteem needs indicate what we need to DO before we feel free to begin to BE the kind of person we can be. This latter represents our self-actualization needs which is where we strive to reach our full potential, unencumbered by material and social needs.

Look at your 8 or so VERY IMPORTANT cards. How many of them are HAVING, DOING, or BEING cards?

The following cards represent each area of need.

HAVING	DOING	BEING
Security	Work with others	Learning
Money	Community	Independence
Routine	Friendship	Creativity
Peace	Contact with People	Challenge
	Recognition	Help Society
	Being Expert	Risk
	Promotion	
	Status	

What does my card sorting tell me about where I am on the hierarchy of needs?

Am I primarily at one level or are my needs distributed throughout the levels?

What does this say about who I am now?

How might I like myself to be different?

NEEDS AND WORK SATISFACTIONS

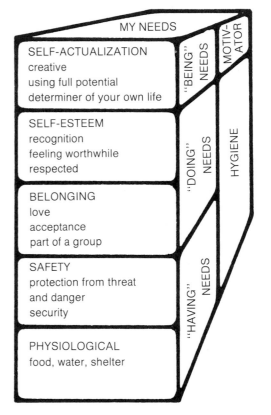

The diagram above sums up what we have been discussing about levels of needs and has added to it an important idea developed from an American behavioural scientist, Frederick Herzberg.

Although originally concerned with paid work only, we believe his theory can apply to unpaid work too. He discovered that what made employees dissatisfied was not always the opposite of what brought them satisfaction. For example, he found that people could get very dissatisfied with problems about:

salary

job security

supervisor behaviour

company policy

but when these were rectified it did not automatically guarantee satisfaction. That only derived from factors present in the job, for example,

achievement

recognition

growth.

Herzberg called the first group 'HYGIENE' factors, because they helped to prevent dissatisfaction but in themselves would never provide real satisfaction. In other words, you can be getting a good salary in a secure job in a company you like and not feel dissatisfied, but not feel satisfied either. For that you need some of the 'MOTIVATOR' elements to be present. This can help to explain to people why sometimes they feel something is missing in their working lives yet they appear to have 'a good job'.

In short, HYGIENE factors can prevent dissatisfaction but only MOTIVATORS can guarantee satisfaction.

Exercise 9: What are my hygiene and motivation factors?

RAINBOW BUILDING SKILL: Knowing yourself

Some researchers have criticized Herzberg saying that it is naive to assume that what is a motivator for one person will be a motivator for everyone, for example, increasing responsibility. We believe strongly that although this criticism might be true it need not take away from the value of the theory. This exercise will enable you to work out for yourself what are your own HYGIENE and MOTIVATOR factors.

- Sort through the Work Values cards. Ask yourself these 2 questions:
  (A) "Which of these causes me irritation or frustration if I don't have them?"
  (B) "Which of these when I do have them makes me feel really fulfilled and involved with my work?

Now sort the cards into 2 piles, according to your answers.

- Write down your answers from your cards.
  List (A) represents YOUR Hygiene factors
  List (B) represents YOUR Motivator factors

Does this suggest anything for my AHA! FOLDER?

Keep a record
- Notes about what I've discovered

FACT   One quarter of British employees feel they have a "bad job", more than in any other western country.

FACT   The proportion of employees in manufacturing industry has now dropped to under 25% (1984).

49

WHO AM I?

> What have you learned about your
> values and needs and
> how they might change?

....

....

....

....

....

....

....

....

....

....

....

....

....

....

....

....

Having looked at what is important to you (your 'values'), the next question is focussed on what you can do well — your abilities or skills.

In our experience many people have difficulty in identifying their skills. Part of this difficulty reflects being brought up in a culture which deals harshly with people who brag, are immodest, or are 'too big for their boots'. Because of this, many people are more skilled in describing what they are poor at, than what they are good at! But, culture not withstanding, we are also not skilled at knowing how to identify the broad range of things we can do well. This is a vital career planning skill. It is essential to know the base of skills on which changes in your lifestyle or career could be built in the future.

You're More Skilled Than You Think

Importance of Transferable Skills

One of the reasons why we are poor at identifying our skills can be traced to the paramount importance of the paid worker role in our lives. Skills are often linked to the jobs we do. Because we are technicians, accountants, social workers, etc., we find it relatively easy to see that we have skills in working with switch-gear, or knowledge of book-keeping systems, or an understanding of how court-orders should be followed up. However, it is often more difficult to dig deeper than these job content skills to discover the underlying skills which are transferable — not only to a variety of other jobs, but also to other life roles.

For example, many of us may have been, albeit temporarily and a long time ago, a waiter or waitress. But it would not be unusual to hear someone who had actually been a waiter for much of his or her working life, when asked what they can do, reply with a statement like 'nothing — I've only been a waiter'. This is because they can see no deeper than the job content skills. In the table on the next page, we see the job content skills for a waiter in the left-hand column and the underlying transferable skills in the other columns defined under Data, People, Things and Ideas.

We chose, for this example, the job of a waiter because it seems like a relatively straightforward job and yet it can convey, quite simply, the idea of what we are looking for in this exercise.

Certainly, a close awareness of the transferable skills involved in the jobs/roles you have been doing might help you make some changes in your career, without necessarily requiring much — or even any — retraining.

FACT There is increasing evidence of a move towards working from home. The Department of Industry is running a pilot project in which disabled workers will be equipped with new technology to enable them to work from home. Rank Xerox have dispersed 150 executives to work for them from home as self-employed, thereby saving the company £5 million a year in office overheads. ICI have over 200 computer programmers home-based.

SKILLS

"NONE – I'VE ONLY BEEN A WAITER"†

JOB CONTENT SKILLS	WORKING WITH DATA	WORKING WITH PEOPLE	WORKING WITH THINGS	WORKING WITH IDEAS
Setting tables			Manipulating items rapidly	Thinking of new table layouts
Seating people		Making people feel welcome		
Taking orders	Explaining menu items. Writing clearly to be understood by others	Helping		
Delivering order to kitchen	Communicating information to others	Checking for under-standing; Maintain relationships		Thinking of new systems for dealing with orders
Serving food	Ability to memorise		Balancing items	
Suggesting desserts	Ability to memorise		Being persuasive	
Checking on satisfaction	Seeking feedback	Listening, caring		
Delivering bill, taking money and providing change	Copying; numeracy	Dealing with people courteously		
Thank them		Dealing with people courteously		

†This has been freely adapted from Richard Bolles, The Three Boxes of Life, Berkeley, Ten Speed Press, 1978.

RAINBOW BUILDING SKILLS: Knowing yourself
                          Research skills

On the following pages headed 'SKILLS DESCRIPTIONS' you will find a number of cards to cut out, as you did for the Work Values exercise.

- Amongst the cards you cut out will be 4 cards with the following words on them:

  VERY COMPETENT
  COMPETENT
  ADEQUATE FOR TASK
  UNDEVELOPED

- Place these 4 cards in front of you. Sort all the rest under them by asking yourself:

> Which of these skills can I perform very competently, competently, adequately, and which have I not yet developed?

- If you believe you have some transferable skills which are not represented on the cards, write on the blank cards provided.

- Write down in the table on Page 61 all the skills at which you assess yourself as VERY COMPETENT and COMPETENT.

- Look at the skills in the COMPETENT, ADEQUATE, and UNDEVELOPED columns. At which of these would you like to become more competent? Write these down in the table.

- Take your VERY COMPETENT and COMPETENT skills and sort them into 3 piles indicating those you:-
  –WANT TO USE A GREAT DEAL
  –WANT TO USE SOMETIMES
  –WANT TO USE RARELY OR NEVER

- The skills you have identified as your VERY COMPETENT ones and WANT TO USE A GREAT DEAL are your most transferable skills.

- The skills you have identified as your COMPETENT and WANT TO USE A GREAT DEAL are your next most transferable skills.

Not wanting to use these skills does not necessarily make them non-transferable. But we have found that people are less likely to want to look for opportunities which involve using skills they are less motivated to use.

- Each of the skill cards has a letter on them:

D I P T

Data, Ideas, People, Things

D = DATA These represent the kind of skills required to record, communicate, evaluate, and organise facts or data about goods and services. People who like using these skills typically enjoy working with figures, systems, and routines.

I = IDEAS These represent skills used in being creative, designing conceptual models and systems, experimenting with words, figures, music. People who like using these skills typically enjoy creating, discovering, interpreting, synthesising and abstract thinking.

P = PEOPLE These represent skills used in helping, informing, teaching, serving, persuading, entertaining, motivating, selling and directing other people. People who use these skills like to work for changes in other people's behaviour.

T = THINGS These represent skills used in making, repairing, transporting, servicing. People with these skills like using tools and machinery and understanding how things work.

> How many of my transferable skills are in each of the categories DATA IDEAS PEOPLE THINGS?

Add these letters to the table on page 61 which lists your transferable skills. Place D I P or T after each skill.

If you turn to the World of Employment Map on page 62 you will see that all areas of employment are located there†. Jobs have been assigned to 24 JOB FAMILIES. A JOB FAMILY is a group of jobs related to one another on the basis of their degree of involvement in working with Data, Ideas, People and Things. The 24 JOB FAMILIES are described in APPENDIX 1 (page 153).

Each JOB FAMILY is located on the World of Employment Map according to how alike it is to the other 23 JOB FAMILIES when compared according to Data, Ideas, People and Things. The map is split into 12 regions. Those regions next to one another have most in common. Those on opposite sides of the circle have least in common.

If you have transferable skills primarily in:

PEOPLE – you might explore jobs in	REGIONS 12 and 1
PEOPLE and DATA – you might explore jobs in	REGION 2
DATA – you might explore jobs in	REGIONS 3 and 4
DATA and THINGS – you might explore jobs in	REGION 5
THINGS – you might explore jobs in	REGIONS 6 and 7
THINGS and IDEAS – you might explore jobs in	REGION 8
IDEAS – you might explore jobs in	REGIONS 9 and 10
IDEAS and PEOPLE – you might explore jobs in	REGION 11

VERY COMPETENT	COMPETENT	ADEQUATE FOR TASK
UNDEVELOPED	P Drawing out people	T Hand – eye co-ordination
T Keeping physically fit	T Using hand tools	T Handling things with precision and speed
T Assembling things	T Fixing, repairing things	D Analysing, dissecting, sorting and sifting through information or things
T Building, constructing	T Muscular co-ordination	D Problem-solving
T Finding out how things work	T Physically strong	D Reviewing, evaluating
T Driving car, motorbike	T Quick physical reactions	D Diagnosing, looking for problems
T Manual dexterity	T Using machine tools, sewing machine, lathe, power tools	D Organising, classifying

SKILLS DESCRIPTIONS

D Reading for facts	D Following instructions, diagrams, blueprints	I Creating, innovating, seeing alternatives
D Researching, gathering information	I Working creatively with colours	I Sizing up a situation or person quickly and accurately
D Manipulating numbers rapidly in mental arithmetic	I Conveying feelings or thoughts through drawing, painting, etc	I Having insight, using intuition
D Calculating, computing	I Fashioning or shaping things or materials	I Reading for ideas
D Memorising numbers	I Working creatively with spaces, shapes or faces	I Developing other's ideas
D Managing money, budgeting	I Composing music	I Conveying feelings or thoughts through body, face and/or voice
D Examining, observing, surveying, an eye for detail and accuracy	I Improvising, adapting	I Writing creatively
D Taking an inventory	I Designing things, events, learning situations	P Conveying warmth and caring

57

P Helping others	P Taking first move in relationships	P Promoting change
P Giving credit to others, showing appreciation	P Motivating people	P Leading, directing others
P Listening	P Organising people	P Showing sensitivity to others' feelings
P Selling, persuading, negotiating	P Teaching, training	P Performing in a group, on stage, in public, etc.

MY TRANSFERABLE SKILLS

VERY COMPETENT	COMPETENT	WANT TO USE A GREAT DEAL	SKILLS I WOULD LIKE TO DEVELOP
		WANT TO USE SOMETIMES	
		WANT TO USE RARELY OR NEVER	

World of Employment Map

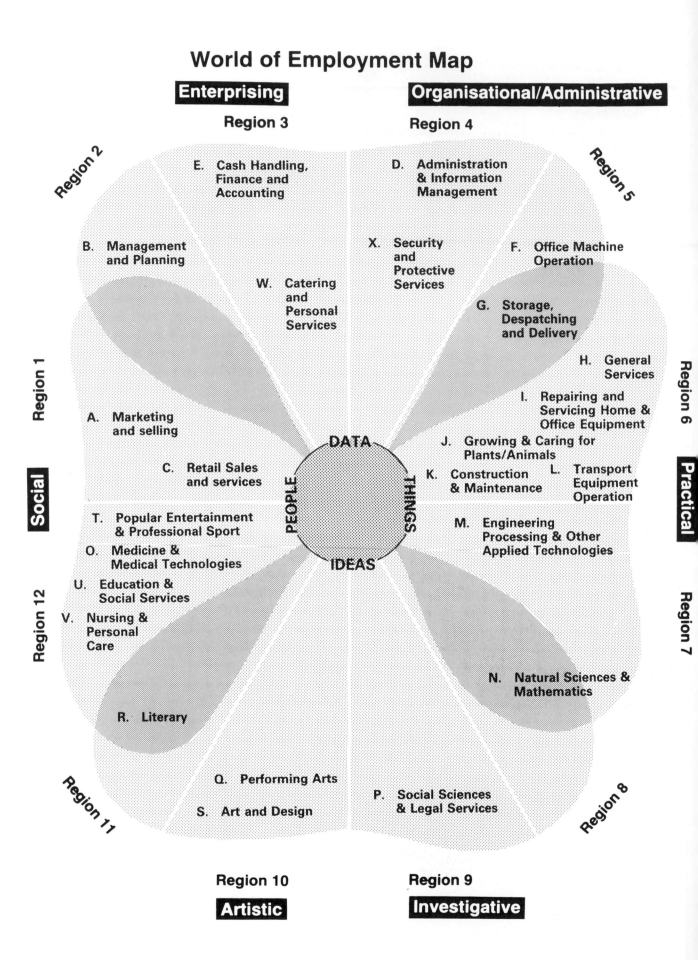

Enterprising

Region 3

Organisational/Administrative

Region 4

Region 2

Region 5

E. Cash Handling, Finance and Accounting

D. Administration & Information Management

B. Management and Planning

X. Security and Protective Services

F. Office Machine Operation

W. Catering and Personal Services

G. Storage, Despatching and Delivery

Region 1

H. General Services

A. Marketing and selling

DATA

I. Repairing and Servicing Home & Office Equipment

J. Growing & Caring for Plants/Animals

Region 6

C. Retail Sales and services

PEOPLE

THINGS

K. Construction & Maintenance

L. Transport Equipment Operation

Social

T. Popular Entertainment & Professional Sport

IDEAS

M. Engineering Processing & Other Applied Technologies

Practical

O. Medicine & Medical Technologies

U. Education & Social Services

Region 12

V. Nursing & Personal Care

Region 7

N. Natural Sciences & Mathematics

R. Literary

Region 11

Q. Performing Arts

S. Art and Design

P. Social Sciences & Legal Services

Region 8

Region 10

Region 9

Artistic

Investigative

Moira Dalgleish

was another participant on one of our workshops.

Moira's skills were primarily in Ideas. The World of Employment Map on page 62 suggests that she would be able to use those skills most in Regions 9 and 10. In those regions are found JOB FAMILIES: Q, P, and S. She looked these up in Appendix 1, having first identified her qualifications level as 2. None of these jobs appealed greatly to her so she looked at the next closest JOB FAMILIES, which were R and N. Out of those N was of the most interest because her next highest group of skills was in THINGS.

This does not mean that Moira <u>must</u> look for a job in these areas. It does mean that with the skills that she has she is most likely to be able to adapt to the skill demands of these jobs.

From the next exercise, however, we shall discover that she has interests which do not coincide exactly with her skills.

Keep a record

- My transferable skills chart.

- My position on the map.

- List of suggested jobs.

FACT 2 out of every 5 employees are women. 3 out of every 5 married women under 60 have jobs.

FACT The number of 16 to 18 year olds available for employment will fall about 25% between June 1987 and June 1995.

The anticipated fall in the number of school leavers is also unevenly spread geographically: the extremes are − 32% in Merseyside; and − 12% in West Sussex; the average for England is − 24.4%.
(Source: Training Commission).

The demographic shrinkage comes on top of existing shortages of skills in key areas: information technology is already short of 20,000 people; on current figures, this will increase to 50,000 by 1991.

Looking at Your Interests

Exercise 11: What are my interests?*

RAINBOW BUILDING SKILL: Knowing yourself

Your interests represent your preferences for doing some activities instead of others. Some people like driving cars, others like exploring caves, some like keeping financial records, while others like drawing diagrams.

This exercise is based on the work of John Holland[9] who discovered that people's interests incline them to particular types of occupation. He also found that people in the same occupation, although they may have different values, will have similar skills and interests.

On this and the next page are 6 sets of statements. For each of them, show how much you agree or disagree with the statement.

1 = Highly disagree
5 = Highly agree

Circle the number that represents your level of agreement.

INTERESTS – GROUP P

1　2　3　4　5　I like fixing and repairing things

1　2　3　4　5　I like to be very fit

1　2　3　4　5　I like making things with my hands
1　2　3　4　5　I like doing things outdoors
1　2　3　4　5　I like hard, physical work
1　2　3　4　5　I feel comfortable working with tools and machines

Add up the numbers　　　　TOTAL FOR P =

INTERESTS – GROUP I

1　2　3　4　5　I like to understand things thoroughly

1　2　3　4　5　I like exploring new ideas

1　2　3　4　5　I enjoy working on problems

1　2　3　4　5　I like asking questions

1　2　3　4　5　I like learning about new things

1　2　3　4　5　I like to work out my own answers to problems

Add up the numbers　　　　TOTAL FOR I =

INTERESTS – GROUP A

1　2　3　4　5　I like seeing art shows, plays and good films

1　2　3　4　5　I like to be different

1　2　3　4　5　I like to forget about everything else when I'm being creative

1　2　3　4　5　It is vital to have beautiful and unusual things around me

1　2　3　4　5　I like to use my imagination

1　2　3　4　5　I like expressing myself on paper, through painting, music, or by building things

----

Add up the numbers　　　　TOTAL FOR A =

INTERESTS – GROUP S

1　2　3　4　5　I enjoy being with people

1　2　3　4　5　I like to talk things through with people

1　2　3　4　5　I like to pay attention to what people want

1　2　3　4　5　I like helping people

1　2　3　4　5　I like helping people to develop and learn things

1　2　3　4　5　Who I'm with is more important than where I am

Add up the numbers　　　　TOTAL FOR S =

INTERESTS – GROUP E

------

1 2 3 4 5   I enjoy trying to persuade and influence people

1 2 3 4 5   I enjoy using a great deal of energy and resilience

1 2 3 4 5   I like people to do what I ask of them

1 2 3 4 5   I like taking risks

1 2 3 4 5   I like making decisions

1 2 3 4 5   I enjoy getting people organised and excited about a task

------

Add up the numbers   TOTAL FOR E =

INTERESTS – GROUP O/A

------

1 2 3 4 5   I like to be given clear directions

1 2 3 4 5   I enjoy getting the details right in my work

1 2 3 4 5   I like a clear structure and a regular routine

1 2 3 4 5   I can be relied upon to do what I'm expected to do

1 2 3 4 5   I enjoy working with figures

1 2 3 4 5   I like organising projects, ideas and people down to the last detail

------

Add up the numbers   TOTAL FOR O/A =

- Rank order the letters P I A S E O / A according to which interest group has the highest and the lowest scores fo you.

- Take your top 3 scores. These represent your 3 majo interest types.

My top group is .... ☐

My second highest group is .... ☐

My third highest group is .... ☐

There follows an interpretation for each interest group.

INTEREST TYPES

PRACTICAL: THINGS FOCUS

These people like to work with tools, objects, machines or animals. They like to develop manual, mechanical, agricultural and electronic skills. They like jobs which involve building and repairing things. They like using their hands. They use their bodies skillfully rather than words, thoughts or feelings. They admire physical co-ordination, strength, agility and logic. They like being outdoors and dealing with concrete problems. They tend to be down to earth and matter of fact. They solve problems by DOING.

INVESTIGATIVE: IDEAS FOCUS

These people enjoy using their minds. They tend to be curious, studious, independent, intellectual, sometimes unconventional, and introspective. They like to develop skills in maths, biology and the physical sciences. They like scientific and medical jobs. They like thinking through problems, trusting their own minds more than other people and things. They admire logic, use insight, enjoy intellectual challenges. They solve problems by THINKING.

ARTISTIC: IDEAS AND PEOPLE FOCUS

These people like to feel free from routine. They like to develop skills in language, art, music, drama and writing. They trust their minds, bodies and feelings, being more suspicious of things. They enjoy beauty, unstructured activity, variety, interesting and unusual sounds, sights, textures and people. They tend to be creative, talented and freewheeling, often non-conformist, sensitive, independent, introspective, expressive. They like jobs where they can use their creative skills. They solve problems by being CREATIVE.

SOCIAL: PEOPLE FOCUS

These people live through their feelings. Relying on gut reactions, they like activities that involve informing, training, teaching, understanding and helping others. They develop skills for working with people. They tend to be helpful, friendly, concerned leaders, sensitive, supportive, responsible, perceptive, genuine, tactful, empathetic. They enjoy being close to people, sharing problems, being in charge, unstructured activities. They like jobs such as teaching, nursing, and counselling. They solve problems by using their FEELINGS.

ENTERPRISING: PEOPLE AND DATA FOCUS

These people love projects. They like leading and influencing people, are often ambitious, outgoing, energetic, self-confident, independent, enthusiastic, sensitive and logical. They develop skills to lead, motivate and persuade people. They enjoy organising, managing, variety, status, power and money. They solve problems, by RISKING themselves and others.

ORGANISATIONAL/ADMINISTRATIVE: DATA AND THINK FOCUS

These people enjoy orderliness and clear routines. They like activities that encourage organising information in a clear and logical way. They tend to be responsible, dependable, careful, logical, and accurate. They have an eye for detail. They enjoy order, security and certainty, identifying with power and status. They develop office and arithmetical skills. They like jobs involving systems, operating computers and word processors. They often like working in large organisations. They solve problems by following ROUTINES.

- Examine the World of Employment Map on page 62. You will see that each interest type corresponds to 2 regions.

Practical	=	Regions 6 and 7
Investigative	=	Regions 8 and 9
Artistic	=	Regions 10 and 11
Social	=	Regions 12 and 1
Enterprising	=	Regions 2 and 3
Organisational/ Administrative	=	Regions 4 and 5

- Put an X in the regions which incorporate your top 3 letters (P I A S E or O/A).

These represent the JOB FAMILIES where people with your kind of interest tend to cluster.

- For a more direct reading of which jobs might be suitable for you according to your interests, look up your 3-letter code in Appendix 2 (page 174). There you will find JOB FAMILY regions classified according to the 3-letter codes. Look at Appendix 1 (page 153). Find the JOB FAMILIES indicated from your 3-letter code, decide on your Level of Entry, and see which jobs match your interests.

FACT 9% of the labour force are now self-employed, and the percentage has increased rapidly over the last five years.

Moira Dalgleish

Moira's 3-letter code was S,I,O, Social, Investigative, and Organisational/Administrative. The Investigative interests (Regions 8 and 9) are consistent with her skills. This means that the jobs in Social Sciences and Legal Services (Q and P) and in the Natural Sciences and Mathematics (N) are likely to be ones she would be both interested in and would be able to do.

Moira's strongest interest, however, was in the Social area (Regions 12 and 1). Just because she does not possess skills which are not immediately and obviously transferable to these jobs does not mean that she should not consider them. It does mean that she needs to think extra carefully about it. But given sufficiently high motivation, people can develop skills in many areas in which they have not yet demonstrated expertise.

Her biggest contrast is between her interests in Regions 4 and 5 (Organisational/Administrative) and her skills which are primarily opposite these regions on the map, in Regions 9 and 10. Again this should not automatically rule out a job choice in Regions 4 and 5, but she would need to analyse the job specifications carefully and ask herself if she is really prepared to put in the work to develop the new skills that clearly would be called upon.

Choosing a leisure pursuit

1. Find your primary interest areas. Check to see the kinds of activity that are typical for people with your interests in Appendix 3 (page 180).

2. Write in the space overleaf your 10 favourite leisure time activities in rank order from your most favourite to your 10th favourite. Include any that you would like to try but may not have tried yet in your life.

3. The columns that follow ask you to fill in details about your leisure activities, for example, can you do it alone or do you need others, does it cost you money, is it energetic, is it risking in any way, etc.

LEISURE ACTIVITY	Alone (A) or with People (P)?	Does it cost £5 or more (£)?	Does it involve risk? Physical (P) Emotional (E) Intellectual (I)	Energetic (E) or Non-energetic (NE)?	Do you do it Often (O) Sometimes (S) Rarely (R)?	When did you last do it?
1.						
2.						
3.						
4.						
5.						
6.						
7.						
8.						
9.						
10.						

What does this say about your leisure life?

For example, on one of our workshops, Kate discovered that she needed a balance of activities involving people and being alone. Dave was not surprised to find a high level of physical risk in his activities (he scored high on Practical and Enterprising). Linda found she rarely did any of the things she enjoyed doing. Jacob realised that his leisure activities cost him almost nothing and Margaret his wife, found 3 activities from Appendix 3 that she had never thought of doing but had now included in her list.

Watch Point

There is some evidence to suggest that our interests determine how we spend our leisure time as well as the kind of paid work we choose to do. In looking up your most likely leisure activities in Appendix 3 you should find the kinds of things that would appeal to you. However, remember that although many people have leisure interests similar to their paid work interests, some people like their leisure interests to appeal to a different aspect of their personality. John, a very successful sales manager who loves his job (Enterprising) as a complete break enjoys building model ships (Practical).

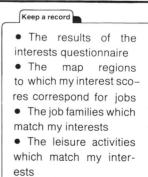

Keep a record

- The results of the interests questionnaire
- The map regions to which my interest scores correspond for jobs
- The job families which match my interests
- The leisure activities which match my interests

WHO AM I?

You have now completed your life review, analysed how you spend your time, identified your work values, discovered your transferable skills, and described your areas of interest. You have also matched your skills and interests against the World of Employment Map to see which job families, educational courses and leisure activities are suited to them.

What have you learned about the types of job which would match your skills and interests?

What have you learned about leisure pursuits in which you might engage?

Choosing Where To Live

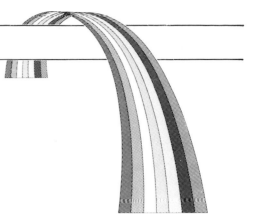

RAINBOW BUILDING SKILLS: Knowing yourself
Research skills

In the past 50 years we have become more mobile than at any time in our history since the waves of invaders prior to 1066.

 The average life of a mortgage in this country is now less than 8 years.

 35% of people moved house at least once during the past 5 years.

 Among professional groups, over 50% moved at least once in the past 5 years, and 20% moved twice or more. Much of the movement, however, is still quite local, and as a nation we are still relatively static when we compare ourselves with the gypsy-style wanderings of the Americans. Yet the reality is that it is a real choice as to where we choose to live. We often take it for granted that we do not have a choice.

RAINBOW BUILDERS ALWAYS HAVE A CHOICE

This exercise is designed to get you to reassess the choice you have and are making by living where you are now. You *can* choose to live elsewhere in our country. It is increasingly easy to live and work in EEC countries, and it is possible to emigrate to other countries – traditionally Australia, New Zealand, Canada, South Africa, the USA, but in theory large parts of the globe.

- On the next page you will see 15 balloons displaying 12 different aspects of qualities of living. There are 3 blank balloons for you to add any aspects important to you but missing from our list. Most of the balloons we think are self-explanatory, but perhaps an explanation of some of them would help you:

  TOWN/COUNTRY = living in either a town or the country is important to you, or some combination of the two.

  PROXIMITY TO FAMILY = the distance you live from relatives and in-laws.

  CULTURAL AMENITIES = availability of theatre, cinema, art galleries, further educational opportunities, restaurants, libraries.

- Rank order on page 70 the balloons in the figure overleaf according to their importance to you. Your most important aspect placed alongside 15, your next most important beside 14, etc.

- Then rate each aspect according to how far that is satisfied by your present place of living by allocating it 0, 1, or 2 in the space provided.

  0 = not satisfied at all
  1 = some satisfaction
  2 = mostly or completely satisfied

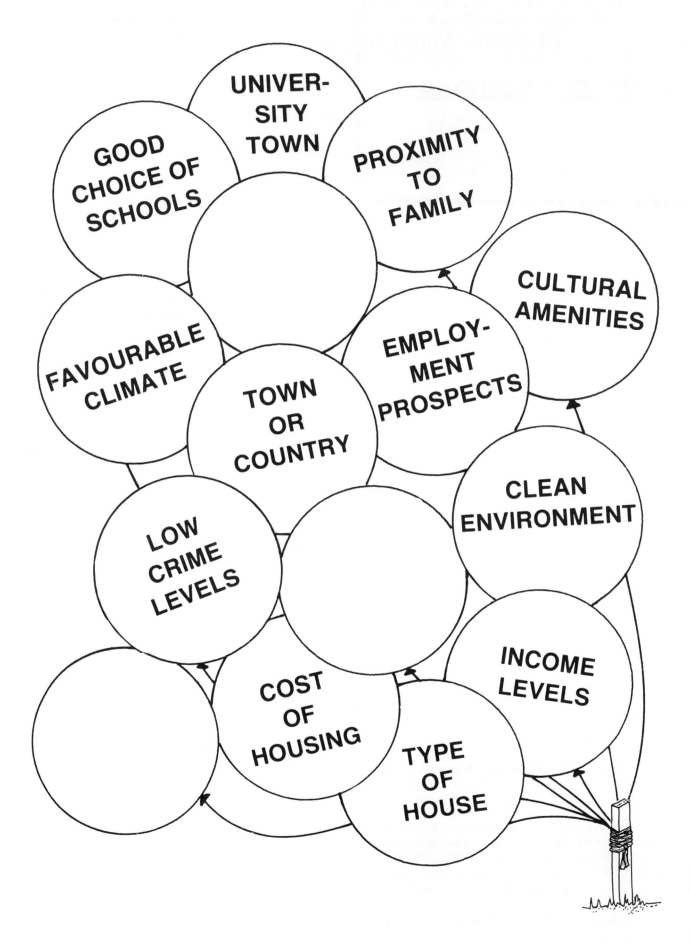

WHAT I WANT FROM WHERE I LIVE
0/1/2

15.............................. x .... = ...

14.............................. x .... = ...

13.............................. x .... = ...

12.............................. x .... = ...

11.............................. x .... = ...

10.............................. x .... = ...

9.............................. x .... = ...

8.............................. x .... = ...

7.............................. x .... = ...

6.............................. x .... = ...

5.............................. x .... = ...

4.............................. x .... = ...

3.............................. x .... = ...

2.............................. x .... = ...

1.............................. x .... = ...

TOTAL POINTS   =

- Multiply your own ranking by the rating from 0-2, as you can see in the example below. Then add up the total. This will give you an indication of how well you see your living needs are being satisfied right now. The maximum total possible is 240, the lowest total possible is 0.

FOR EXAMPLE

15	Favourable Climate	x 0	=	0
14	Town/Country	x 2	=	28
13	Clean Environment	x 1	=	13
12	Low Crime Levels	x 1	=	12

- The following will give you some indication of what your scores mean

180-240 Well matched. Probably enjoy where you're living. Little reason to look for a change.

140-179 Quite well matched. Some things missing which will need compensating for. Not much of an incentive to move.

100-139 Adequate. You will often think about moving but probably won't.

60-99 Inadequate. This leaves much to be desired about where you live. You should seriously be questioning whether you should stay. What in particular are you not getting? Is it a widespread dissatisfaction or just related to a few outstanding absences?

Below 60 Do you really want to stay???

- You can, of course, use your rankings to compare your present living place with other places in the country to which you might consider moving.

Keep a record

- The results of the ranking and rating exercise.
- Notes about the sorts of living situation/locations which might suit you better.

Rainbow Building Summary Sheet

WHO AM I?

My major PAID WORK VALUES are:

....
....
....
....
....
....
....
....
....
....
....
....

My major UNPAID WORK VALUES are:

....
....
....
....
....
....
....
....
....
....
....
....

My TRANSFERABLE SKILLS are in:

PEOPLE

DATA

IDEAS

THINGS

(Circle)

My major INTERESTS are:

P

I

A

E

S

O/A

(Circle)

My major TRANSFERABLE SKILLS are:

....
....
....
....
....
....
....
....

I want to LIVE somewhere that has the following attributes (in order):

....
....
....
....
....
....
....
....

Question 2
WHERE AM I NOW?

Having identified your skills, values and interests, and knowing something about your preferred lifestyle, it is now time to stop and examine where you are on your journey through life.

ROUTE MAP for "Where am I now?"

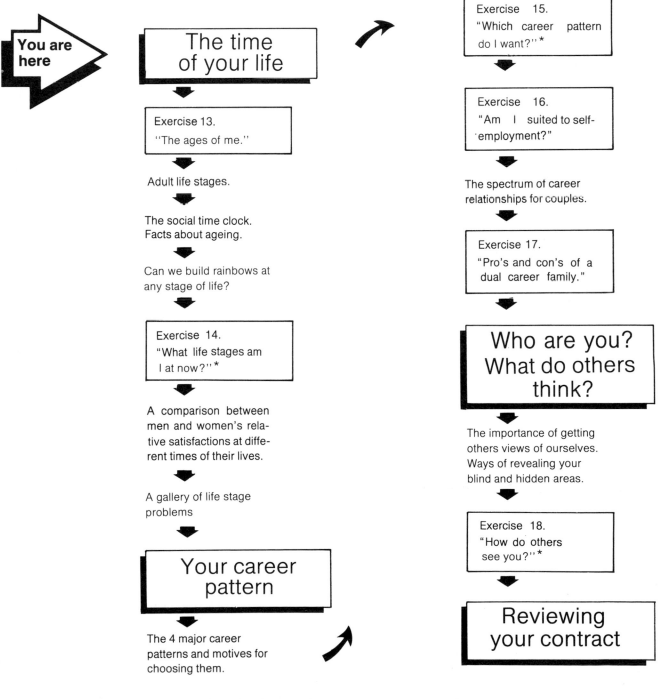

You are here

The time of your life

Exercise 13.
"The ages of me."

Adult life stages.

The social time clock.
Facts about ageing.

Can we build rainbows at any stage of life?

Exercise 14.
"What life stages am I at now?" *

A comparison between men and women's relative satisfactions at different times of their lives.

A gallery of life stage problems

Your career pattern

The 4 major career patterns and motives for choosing them.

Exercise 15.
"Which career pattern do I want?" *

Exercise 16.
"Am I suited to self-employment?"

The spectrum of career relationships for couples.

Exercise 17.
"Pro's and con's of a dual career family."

Who are you? What do others think?

The importance of getting others views of ourselves. Ways of revealing your blind and hidden areas.

Exercise 18.
"How do others see you?" *

Reviewing your contract

The Time Of Your Life

RAINBOW BUILDING SKILL: Knowing yourself

- Fill in the gaps in the following sentences

    1. In other people's eyes, I look as though I am about .... years of age.

    2. In my own eyes, I judge my body to be like that of a person of about .... years of age.

    3. My thoughts and interests are like those of a person about .... years of age.

    4. My position in society is like that of a person about .... years of age.

    5. Deep down inside, I really feel like a person about .... years of age.

    And just one more question:

    6. I would honestly prefer to be about .... years of age.

> What do my answers say about me and how I see myself?
>
> What does it say about how I regard ageing?

Probably, if you are like most people, you will not have given the same age for all the questions. That is because age is so very much more than a biological process. It is highly charged with social and emotional significance.

One of the most typical differences in people's answers occurs between 'feel' and chronological ages. People in their third decade and beyond usually 'feel' younger than their 'official' age. This remains true of many people in their 70s and 80s.

It has been found that most people in their third decade and beyond prefer to be younger than their actual chronological age. Very rarely, however, do people actually express a preference for being older, except for some young teenagers.

It is tempting to shrug and say, 'Well, that is just about what we would expect, isn't it?' But why is this just what we would expect? The fact is that many people do have an aversion to old age, but ageing does not have to be a negative experience, and in many cultures is not.

What is known about Adult life stages?

Modern developmental psychology is notorious for its preoccupation with infancy and adolescence and its neglect of adulthood. Until 10 years ago to look at a typical textbook in psychology you could think that human development stopped at age 21. Fortunately writers and philosophers have been more observant, more introspective, and less timid in exploring the longest period of our lives. The Talmud, 2500 years ago, in the 'Sayings of the Fathers', outlined 14 ages of Man, complete with developmental tasks! Confucius in 500 BC identified 6 steps in the life cycle, while the Greek poet Solon in 700 BC divided life into ten stages, each lasting 7 years. More recently, and better known, Shakespeare in "As You Like It" outlined seven ages of man. But until the 1970s there was almost complete silence from behavioural scientists about the experience of being adult. Daniel Levinson[10] has described the nature of adult life as 'one of the best-kept secrets in our society, and probably in human history generally'.

One of the consequences of this is that people in general have often assumed a stability in adult life which recent research has demonstrated to be the exception rather than the rule. People so quickly negate their own experience when they believe that the experience is probably unique and so the myth continues.

Yet alongside the concept of stability is a clear identification in many people's eyes of what is appropriate behaviour for one's age. In other words there is an implicit understanding of different stages of life – the experimentation of adolescence, the settling down into a job and marriage, becoming parents then grandparents, and finally, retirement. The different tasks which accompany these events are talked about, but the psychological changes concommitant with them much less so. Consequently myths develop about the different age groups, e.g. young adults under 25 are supposed to be autonomous, exuberant, high in drive to achieve and be reluctant to be "looked after". Therefore, when 25 year old men and women find themselves apathetic, tired and depressed by the limited circumstances of their lives, they are doubly depressed – by their actual life situation plus the feeling that people of their age should not be like this. They feel they cannot ask for help from

† Adapted from Robert Kastenbaum, GROWING OLD, Harper and Row, 1979.

others because they are supposed to be independent. If they enjoy being quiet, low-achievers they suspect that there must be something wrong with them. All too often they jump into roles that they think they 'should' be ready for – deciding on a long-term career, getting married, having children – when clearly they are not ready.

Similarly, the myth of the middle years is that adults are responsible, settled, contented, at the peak of their achievements. But what of the adults in this group who find that instead of being content with their responsibilities they wish to explore new experiences, try new careers, new styles of living?

At 60 to 65 people are supposed to become 'old' – ready to retire, lose their health, their wits and their income, be dependent on their children, to be hopeless and unattractive. But what if they are fully fit, alert, fall in love with someone new, want a divorce, act out a lifelong ambition to travel round the world, etc?

The social time clock

Bernice Neugarten[11] has suggested that 'there exists a socially prescribed timetable for the ordering of major life events' and that most adults conform to this timetable. Remarkable agreement has been found in the general population regarding what age is appropriate for particular behaviour. For example, 4 in 5 believed that a man should marry between 20 and 25 and a woman between 19 and 24; that people should finish their education and get a job between 20 and 22; retire between 60 and 65. It is as if there is a social time clock which regulates our lives, by which we judge whether we are 'on-time' for certain things in our lives.

To be 'off-time', whether early or late, is to be an age deviant. Like any other kind of deviance, this carries with it social penalties. The woman not married by age 29 used to – and maybe still does – feel embarrassed by it. The man who returns to college at 45 can feel and be treated as peculiar. It can be as shameful to have a baby at age 45 as at age 15.

It does seem that it is harder for a person to go against age expectations in their 20's than in their 40's.

The evidence clearly suggests that there are strong culturally transmitted expectations of behaviour relating to adulthood. This makes people feel good if they are 'on-time' and bad if they are 'off-time'. But what is the empirical evidence for some of these age-bound expectations?

Changes in adulthood: The facts[12]

Physical development
The range of individual differences is enormous and no physical change during adulthood can be exactly predicted from chronological age – the one possible exception being grey hair! Longevity and youthfulness run in families and are also more class than age related. People from lower socio-economic groups tend to age faster and die sooner than those from middle and upper socio-economic groups, and to suffer from poorer health throughout their lives. There follows a list of findings:

- maximum height is attained at the beginning of adulthood;

- strength peaks between 25 and 30, after which the muscles – especially in the back and the legs – weaken somewhat unless maintained by exercise;

- manual dexterity is greatest at about 33;

- sight diminishes throughout adulthood;

- in middle age people tend to put on weight around the waist and hips;

- there is gradual hearing loss after 20, especially among men;

- sensitivity to smell decreases at 40;

- sensitivity to taste diminishes after 50;

- appearance alters at middle age – hair greys and recedes, skin coarsens and darkens, wrinkles appear;

- adults get fewer acute illnesses and more chronic ones than children;

- older adults take longer to recuperate from illness;

- sexual potency reaches its peak in late adolescence for men and in the mid-twenties for women;†

- women cease menstruation at 40-50.

Intellectual development
It used to be thought by psychologists that intelligence followed an inverted U-shaped curve, peaking in the mid-20's, then declining. However, once the different dimensions of 'intelligence' are examined the picture looks very different:

- the capacity for rapid processing of information in problem solving ('fluid intelligence') declines steadily from the late teens;

- 'crystallised intelligence' which relates to the storage of information such as vocabulary and general knowledge, increases over the adult years;

- short-term memory is variable but long-term memory remains stable, especially with practice;

- problem solving and reasoning may deteriorate slightly with age, especially when speed is called for;

- creative output varies widely according to the subject – chemists and mathematicians have tended to peak in their 20's and 30's, novelists in their 40's and 50's, poets in their 20's, architects in their late 40's.

Motivation is obviously a key factor and older people may learn more – and learn it better – because they want more intensely to learn and so work harder at it.

†Potency, of course, relates to quantity not quality!

Can we build RAINBOWS at any stage of life?

Yes, but they will probably look very different at different stages.

We have already discussed the widespread ignorance of adult development from an empirical viewpoint until the 1970's. Then came the work of Levinson [10], Sheehy [2] and others. We have combined these studies to produce the following table.

STAGES AND TASKS OF ADULTHOOD

STAGES	AGES	TASK
	— 16 —	
PULLING UP ROOTS		Autonomy
		Self-sufficiency
	— 20 —	
PROVISIONAL ADULTHOOD		Select career, make relationships
		Achieve place in society
	— 28 —	
AGE 30 TRANSITION		Search for identity and meaning in life
		Re-assess future objectives
	— 32 —	
ROOTING		Establish long term goals, get career recognition
	— 39 —	
MID-LIFE TRANSITION		Re-examination of career and personal relationships.
		Assess gap between achievement and aspirations.
	— 45 —	
RESTABILISATION and FLOWERING		Autonomy
		Acceptance of time as finite
	— 55 —	
MELLOWING AND RENEWAL		Acceptance of what one has.
		Fewer personal relationships.
		Enjoyment of here-and-now.
	— 65+ —	

Exercise 14: What life stage am I at now?*

RAINBOW BUILDING SKILL: Knowing yourself

- Below you will see eight sentence stems regarding various aspects of your life.

  Circle the *letter* (a, b, c, d, e, f, g) which you feel most accurately describes you currently as you see yourself. Your response should be on the basis of how you think things really are, not how you would like them to be.

  In some cases, more than one statement may describe your current situation. However, you are to select the one statement which is *most* characteristic of you.

Adult Life Stage Questionnaire†

1. My main concern is:

   a. becoming a contributing member of my chosen profession

   b. financial security for retirement purposes

   c. being able to fend for myself

   d. accepting what I have not achieved with my life

   e. taking advantage of my last chance to make it big

   f. selecting the right career

   g. finding out what I want out of life

2. My interpersonal relationships are characterised by:

   a. turmoil and change often being caused by my wanting to find out more about myself

   b. a desire for confirmation of my life choices

   c. a lack of excitement but a need for support; achieving recognition in my career

   d. stability and a sense of well-being

   e. being less intense

   f. a need for support from my close friends

   g. a re-awakening of my old dependent-independent feelings

3. One of my dominant goals is:

   a. really enjoying the here-and-now

   b. achieving independence from my parents

   c. identifying what my life means to me and what I can do with the limited time I have left

   d. deciding what to do with my life

†This exercise has been adapted from the Development Stage Assessment Questionnaire produced by Sperry, Michelson and Hunsaker[13].

   e. making enough money to do what I want

   f. discovering what is right for me

   g. being active socially

4. My primary value is:

   a. security

   b. autonomy

   c. accomplishment/prestige

   d. independence

   e. self-identity

   f. commitment

   g. wisdom

5. My life is:

   a. full of urgency to succeed

   b. not so rushed; it is a time for sharing human experiences

   c. a complete open book; anything could happen

   d. stable; what has been done, has been done

   e. for me to define and control

   f. passing too quickly; I have one last chance to make it

   g. uncertain and full of crucial decisions

6. The future is:

   a. uncertain and becoming increasingly important

   b. full of possibilities

   c. pressing in on me and I am running out of opportunities

   d. not as important as the present

   e. not important

   f. a time I fantasise about

   g. limited and I feel a time squeeze

7. My career behaviour is characterised by:

   a. having conflicts between my career and other demands in my life

   b. getting my career into its proper perspective

   c. learning about the world of employment

   d. reviewing what I want from my career

   e. becoming more effective at what I do

   f. a concern for being remembered when I retire

g. discovering my skills

8. My identity is:

   a. defined by how well I perform in my job

   b. torn between what I am now and wanting to change

   c. well-established with a feeling of relief

   d. well-defined and I am satisfied

   e. still tied up with my family

   f. well-defined even though I may not be completely satisfied with it

   g. something which I don't seem to have control of

Enter the letters you have circled in the table below.

What the Adult life stage exercise can tell you

Knowing your optimum stage of development, and the tasks characteristic of that stage, can tell you whether you are typical of other adults of a comparable age. If your assessment places you in a category that is different from what other adults of a comparable age are experiencing – i.e. you are ahead of or behind others in your development – your discomfort may be the result of having to deal with inappropriate tasks. If your stage of development places you in the appropriate age grouping, your feelings of distress may be caused by a questioning of your life's goals and beliefs, which are characteristic of each development stage. Such information can help you cope with your life-tasks and can help show you what needs to be done to get through that stage.

While each stage is general and reflects averages, differences do appear in our development. The common denominator of the changes we experience is what we face not how we face it. What this exercise can help you to determine is:

1. Life tasks appropriate to your stage of development.

2. What obstacles you need to overcome.

3. That your feelings of distress may be 'normal', and that you just need to 'stay with it'.

4. That your feelings of distress are not necessarily caused by your organisation or by some "wrong" decision you made.

The Stages of Adulthood

The following are features of the different life stages:

Provisional Adulthood (Ages 20-28)

During this stage, we are 'out' on our own and are making our first commitments to work, marriage and family, and other adult responsibilities. During provisional adulthood, we first put to use all of the parental upbringing, education and advice that was part of our childhood and adolescence. Rarely analyzing commitments, it is time to explore the real world of career, marriage and lifestyle.

SCORING THE ADULT LIFE STAGE EXERCISE
STAGES OF ADULT DEVELOPMENT

Item	Pulling-up roots (16–20)	Provisional adulthood (20–28)	Age 30 transition (28–32)	Rooting (32–39)	Mid-life transition (39–45)	Restabilization and flowering (45–55)	Mellowing (55–65+)
1	c	f	g	a	e	d	b
2	f	b	a	c	g	d	e
3	b	d	f	e	c	g	a
4	d	f	e	c	b	a	g
5	c	e	g	a	f	d	b
6	f	b	a	g	c	d	e
7	c	g	a	e	d	b	f
8	e	f	g	a	b	c	d
Total no. of items circled in each column	___	___	___	___	___	___	___

The column with the highest frequency of circled items indicates the stage of adult development most characteristic of you now. You will probably find that your scores range across many of the life stages.

Age – 30 Transition (Ages 28 – 32)

During this transition stage, initial commitments of our life-style are often re-examined and their meanings questioned. The surface bravado of the provisional period wavers as life begins to look more complex. Many times we will become impatient with the early choices we made and will feel a new vitality springing from within to answer the question 'What do I really want out of life?' Careers and marriages become particularly vulnerable to reassessment. Long-range implications of continuing with current career, community, and life-style are challenged. In many people change will occur, and in many others there will be a renewed commitment and reaffirmation of their current career, life style and community. This is often a particularly difficult time for women in our present period of history.

Rooting (Ages 32 – 39)

After going through the age-30 transition, we often tend to get our heads down and get on with life. It is a time when we might seek a mentor – a patron or supporter to show us the ropes. Then at about age 35, the time-squeeze begins. Perhaps it is the first emotional awareness that death will come and that time is running out. We now want more than ever to become established. When we start a career or family, we launch them with certain goals and dreams. Some of these are attainable and desirable and others are not. This time-squeeze during the rooting process often begins to worry us. 'Is there still time to change?'

Midlife Transition (Ages 39 – 45)

This is a period which for many has been labelled as midcareer or midlife crisis. It is often a period of acute personal discomfort in which we may face the gap between youthful dreams and actual fulfilments.

Likely limits of success and achievement become more apparent. There may be a difference between what we have reached and what we want. For some people, this transition is merely a decade milestone. For others, it can be a painful time of crisis. It is a lonely time, because each person is ultimately alone on the journey. Children are growing up and going away, and for many their parents are now looking to them for support. We ask many self-searching questions in this period, such as 'What's in it for me?' 'Where am I having fun?' 'Why can't I be accepted for what I am, not what "they" (spouse, boss, society) expect me to be?' 'Is there one last chance to make it big?' In the search for answers that often consumes the midlife transition period, we may turn to a new career or other new directions in life. We may live out life dramas that we haven't yet finished, or that we refuse to allow to lie down and die.

Restabilization and Flowering (Ages 45 – 55)

Once we have gone through the midlife transition, faced mortality, and forged a new life-style, this stage can feel like the best time of life. Often unrushed by the sense of urgency of the thirties, a new stability can be achieved. A career often takes a sharp turn upward. Money becomes less important. Life can become more stable because we listen more to the inner voice than to external demands. We may experience increasing attention to a few old values and a few friends. One hypothesis is that in this and the next stage, if we lose a spouse or close friend, we may go back into provisional-adulthood patterns, trying out life options all over again.

Mellowing and Renewal (Ages 55 – 65+)

At this stage, people tend to become more satisfied with themselves, coming to grips with what they have and haven't done. At first, there is little concern with either past or future, but eventually questions arise as to when to retire, what to do, and how to cope with sudden changes in life-style. It is a difficult step because nearly all of our life is attuned to paid work. Thus an abrupt shift to leisure is sometimes traumatic. The impact of this decision can be compounded by ageing, termination of long-time associations and friendships, and frequently by a total lack of preparation.

Watch Point

Be wary of 'stage theories' that tell you what you should be doing, thinking or feeling at any particular time. Life is not as neat as that. We can be largely restabilizing and flowering but also be dealing with some leftover mid-life transition issues, or even some rooting.

The value of research like this is not to create new psychological and behavioural strait jackets for us, but to let us know that the changes and complexity we might be experiencing are not being experienced in isolation. But although the process is valid enough in general there will be considerable individual differences.

Likewise, the process described now belongs to this historical epoch. It would be rash to presume that fifty years from now, within a different society with likely new concepts of work, leisure, and the family, that the stages would be as they are described here.

Gail Sheehy in her book Pathfinders, did a nationwide (USA) survey of reported satisfaction from men and women which produced some fascinating differences. The table on page 80 summarises her findings.

From a careful examination of this table it is clear that the many conflicting pressures on contemporary women summed up by the dilemma "employment vs. child rearing", are reflected by her findings that from their late 20's women get increasingly dissatisfied with life and only catch up again with men in their early 50's. Her research also suggests that women take longer to resolve their mid-life transitions than men, causing an uncomfortable "diamond" shape between 40-55 on the figure. This represents a period when the sexes are furthest apart in terms of life satisfactions.

Women only really became happier than men at the end of their lives, (presumably after many of the men have died!) The pressures on marriages in mid-life are summarised in the table on page 81.

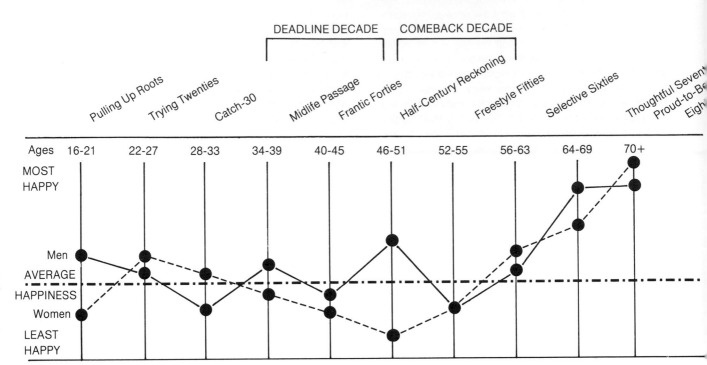

THE HAPPIEST YEARS
A COMPARISON BETWEEN MEN (—) AND WOMEN (– –)

DEADLINE DECADE   COMEBACK DECADE

Pulling Up Roots   Trying Twenties   Catch-30   Midlife Passage   Frantic Forties   Half-Century Reckoning   Freestyle Fifties   Selective Sixties   Thoughtful Seventies Proud-to-Be Eighties

| Ages | 16-21 | 22-27 | 28-33 | 34-39 | 40-45 | 46-51 | 52-55 | 56-63 | 64-69 | 70+ |

MOST
HAPPY

Men
AVERAGE
HAPPINESS
Women

LEAST
HAPPY

Reproduced with permission from Gail Sheehy, *Pathfinders,* Sidgwick & Jackson, 1983.

 On average, women are likely to be out of employment for a total of around 7 years only when forming a family.

 Married men with an economically active wife and two dependent children make up only 5% of all households.

FACT Female employees are absent for 7.7 days per year and males for 7.4 days.

Keep a record
• Your scores from the life stage question-naire
• Notes about how your findings from the questionnaire compare with your actual age and feelings.

ONE TYPICAL FORM OF A MARRIAGE CRISIS AT MIDLIFE

AGES	WIFE	HUSBAND		WIFE	HUSBAND
25-35	Vicariously enjoys husband's career and its rewards, while providing support. Suppresses feelings and:	Suppresses feelings and focusses energy on career achievement.	35-40	Children grow up. She decides vicarious rewards aren't really worth it and begins to feel 'used'. She withdraws support and puts energy into personal growth and achievement for herself. She begins to discover ambition.	He has either accomplished all his goals or discovers he can't; in either case he ends up saying, "Is there nothing more?" His suppressed feelings explode. His need for support sky-rockets. He begins to rediscover feelings.

GIVES ▼   GETS ▲

Emotional,
Housekeeping,
Maternal,
and Sexual
Support

Money
Status
Security
Children

	WIFE	HUSBAND
At age 40-45 leads to	Leads her to think: "Why can't he pull himself together like a good husband so I can go out and develop myself without feeling guilty?"	Leads him to think: "What the hell is she doing running off in other directions while I'm falling apart?"

EXPLOSION IN THE MARRIAGE

Marcel Proust in his book 'Remembrance of Things Past' noted that everyone of us:

"is a creature without any fixed age who has... the faculty of becoming, in a few seconds, many years younger, and who, surrounded by the walls of the time through which he has lived, floats within them but as though in a basin the surface level of which is constantly changing, so as to bring him into the range now of one epoch, now of another."

Daniel Levinson expanding on this theme says that:

"only after we understand the profound significance of the epochs in our lives... can we understand the ways in which one is, at a single time, a child, a youth, a middle-aged and an elderly person. We are never ageless. As we gain a greater sense of our own biographies, however, we can begin to exist at multiple ages. In the process we do not fragment ourselves, rather we become more integrated and whole."

Do I recognise myself?

There follow 5 pictures which represent some of the most common life stage problems we encounter when working with people in organisations.

The important thing to remember is that all of these problems are normal.

That does not mean that your uniqueness is in any way reduced, but it might help to see yourself in perspective. All of these people are desperately in need of RAINBOWS. By working through this book they could all create opportunities for themselves to build some.

SALLY SECRETARY
34 years old

"I really could do an administrative/ supervisory job – couldn't I?"

"I do seem to have as many skills as a lot of my so-called bosses".

"My boss keeps pushing me to be more ambitious".

"Is it worth it when I would have to move if and when my husband moves?"

"My husband wouldn't mind as long as it doesn't affect him or the children".

SUCCESS CHART

PETER PLATEAU
45 years old

"Why am I always being passed over?"

"Why doesn't my boss give me challenging assignments?"

"Just what do you have to do to get promoted around here?"

"Why can't my wife and I communicate?"

"Why do my children seem to believe in everything I don't?"

WHERE AM I NOW?

What did you learn from the adult life
stage questionnaire?

What have you learned about your
'life stage problems'?
Do you have any?

....
....
....
....
....
....
....
....
....
....
....
....
....
....
....
....

Your Career Pattern

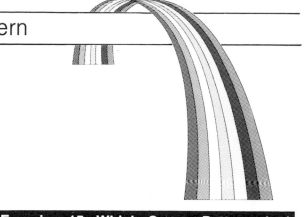

Just as the concept of WORK is changing dramatically, so and not surprisingly, is our concept of CAREER.

Traditionally the word career has come to mean a succession of jobs each of which has higher status than its predecessor with a progressively rising income. This usage became so current that people who did not progress in this way were sometimes referred to as merely having "jobs", while those who did progress had "careers".

We can now recognise that it makes more sense to distinguish between a variety of CAREER PATTERNS.

Following the work in the United States of Michael Driver, we would distinguish between 4 major career patterns from which people tend to choose. The diagram overleaf describes the 4 patterns, states at what life stages this choice tends to be made, the frequency of occupational changes that the people – given the choice – would make, and the directions of the career pattern viewed in hierarchial terms. It also summarises the motives behind the choice of pattern.

These people are examples of the different patterns:

HORIZONTAL
John
(40 years old)

"I've never had a job for more than two years. I get bored. I don't always leave for more money. Sometimes I've earned less. But I like learning new things, meeting new people – it's interesting. I don't suppose I'll ever change now. Some people think my jobs are 'dead-end jobs', but I reckon some of those folks who spend all their lives working their way up are half-dead by the time they get there."

STEADY
Carol
(30 years old)

"I've always wanted to be a nurse. Even before I went to school I had a nurse's uniform. It would be nice to get to be a sister but I'm not really bothered. I'd hate to be a matron – all that book work and responsibility, and you don't have the same relationships with your patients. I'll do this until they kick me out."

VERTICAL
Charles
(55 years old)

"I always wanted a good job with prospects. I've always been ambitious, and I've done well. I had to swap firms a bit during my 30's and 40's but each one moved me up a rung or two. I like the responsibility now. I like making decisions."

CYCLICAL
Janette
(49 years old)

"I really like to get involved in what I'm doing, but I do like learning new things. I made a vow to myself in my 20's that no matter how well I was doing, every 5 five years or so I'd take a good hard look and see if it was still exciting me. If not, I change. I've changed occupations 3 times now and don't regret one of them. I hope to do at least two more very different jobs before I die."

Exercise 15: Which Career Pattern do I want?*

Look at the table on the next page and then answer these questions.

> Which career pattern is closest to the one I've had?

Circle your choice.

HORIZONTAL

STEADY

VERTICAL

CYCLICAL

> Which is the closest to the one I would like in the future?

Circle your choice.

HORIZONTAL

STEADY

VERTICAL

CYCLICAL

CAREER PATTERNS

TYPE OF CAREER	WHEN CHOICE OF PATTERN IS MADE	HOW OFTEN OCCUPATIONS ARE CHANGED	DIRECTION OF CHANGE	MOTIVE FOR CHOOSING THIS PATTERN
HORIZONTAL "VARIETY"	Never. People do not consciously make a choice"	1-2 years	Levels are not relevant	Variety, challenge, "doing what you want to do, regardless"
STEADY "MORE OF THE SAME"	Teenage choice	Never or rarely unless forced	Stays the same	Security, intrinsic job satisfaction, wanting "a job for life"
VERTICAL "THE LADDER"	Teenage choice	Never or rarely unless forced. Jobs are changed for advancement	Upwards	Achievement, status, material success, power
CYCLICAL "THE 5 YEAR ITCH"	Every 5 to 10 years	5-10 years	Levels are not relevant	Variety, personal growth

There are many other decisions to be made about career patterns prior to the one represented by the options of the 4 major types in the diagram. You will be asked to think some more about this.

DECISION 1. Do I want to work full-time or part-time?

Part-time work is increasing rapidly. It has been affected less than full-time employment by the recession and the shift from an Industrial to a Post-Industrial Economy.

 25% of the employed population presently are part-time.

To some extent this is misleading. What we are really seeing is a change in our concept of employment. People are beginning to ask themselves for how many hours they wish to perform paid work each week, or even, in a year. The average working week is reducing, albeit slowly, so that we can anticipate a future where people will do paid work from a range of a few hours to 50 hours a week for a few weeks to almost every week of the year, for a number of years to a full lifetime.

Exercise 16. Am I suited to self employment?†

DECISION 2. Will I be employed by someone else or will I work for myself?

The fastest growing area of the economy is self-employment. There has been almost a 30% increase in the past ten years. The enormous growth of the "black economy" also demonstrates how many people like to work for themselves.

The majority of new jobs are being created in small businesses. We can no longer look to large companies to provide the nation with new jobs. To expand and develop they have to shed labour not increase it.

 In the UK every month 10,000 new businesses are set up. However, only 3 out of 4 survive the first year and only 1 in 5 will be there after 4 years if recent trends continue.

- Here are some arguments for and against self-employment. Put a tick in the box if you are attracted by what it says, a cross if you don't like the idea.

A By being self-employed...

1 I would be my own boss
2 I could work when I wanted to and stop when I felt like it
3 I could use my own money to do something useful
4 I would be free and independent
5 I would learn about business
6 I would improve my self-confidence
7 I would be able to work day and night at something I like doing
8 I would avoid being unemployed and all the problems that go with it
9 I would welcome the chance to think up an idea for a business
10 I would have to make plans
11 I would have to organise my time carefully
12 I would be able to make money out of an idea I've got
13 I could make a lot of money
14 It would give me experiences which I could use later in life
15 I could look for other jobs while working as a self-employed person

How many ticks did you score out of 15?

B By being self-employed...

1 I would have to work on my own a lot
2 I might have to spend all my savings
3 I would have to start work early every morning
4 I would probably have to work in the evenings
5 I would have to organise myself and my work very carefully
6 I would have to persuade other people to help me
7 I would have to sell things or ideas to strangers
8 I would have to find premises or run the business away from home
9 I would have to give up a wage or a benefit which I could receive each week
10 I may have to borrow money from the family or the bank
11 I may have to give up a regular job
12 I may have to go to an evening class to learn business skills
13 I would have to find out if there's any kind of need or demand for my skill or product
14 I would have to find out how to keep business records
15 I would have to work very hard

How many ticks did you score?

87

†This is adapted with permission from Your Own Business, Hobson's Press, 1983.

If you scored 11 to 15 ticks in 'A', then you are clearly the type to be attracted by the idea of working on your own account. If you scored between 8 and 11, you are drawn to the idea, but should find out more about it. If you scored 7 ticks or less, you are the cautious type.

On 'B', if you have 10 to 15 ticks, you are prepared to go on with the idea, even though you see how difficult it could be. If you scored between 6 and 10 ticks, you are interested, but still anxious. If you ticked 5 or less, and put a lot of crosses, you'd be better off in a regular job.

What was your overall score, adding the total for 'A' to the total for 'B'? If you scored 20 ticks out of a possible 30, self-employment could well be the route for you. If you try these tests again in a year's time, you could score very differently.

Decision 3. Am I or will I be part of a dual career family?

We believe strongly in the value of a couple doing this programme together. This actually becomes essential if both partners have jobs. Couples are beginning to discover that having a dual-career family can offer greater opportunities for each individual than if either was the sole breadwinner. It makes sense to decide what income is required as a family and then examine the various alternatives. This can then enable both partners to share more in parenting if they wish or to develop other interests and unpaid work skills that possessing a full-time job would inhibit.

Real life examples have included:
  Both partners taking part-time jobs
  1 partner taking a year off to do other things
  1 partner decreasing his/her job to 75% to provide time for other activities.

The figure below shows a wide spectrum of career relationships possible within the context of a marriage.

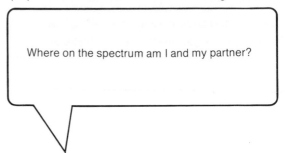

Where on the spectrum am I and my partner?

This figure makes it clear that we should not always take for granted what people mean when they say that they are a "dual-career family". The majority of such couples may have dual careers but they may not have an egalitarian relationship when it comes to domestic responsibilities.

 20% of households now have the wife as the principal earner.

A SPECTRUM OF RELATIONSHIPS FOR COUPLES

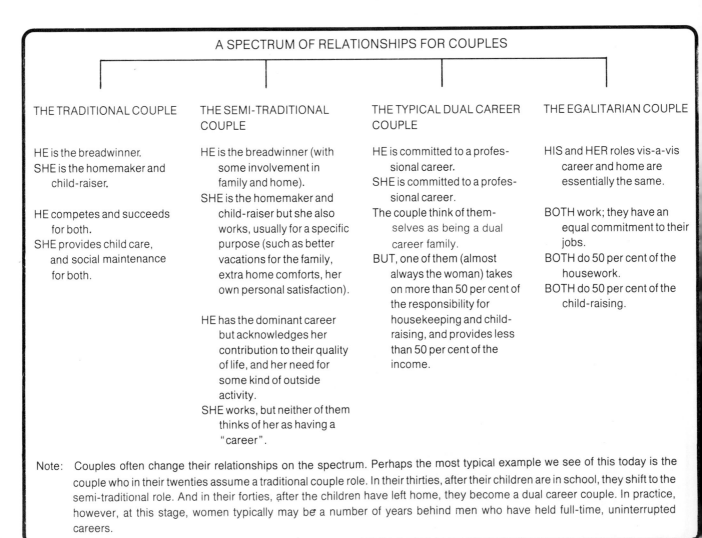

THE TRADITIONAL COUPLE	THE SEMI-TRADITIONAL COUPLE	THE TYPICAL DUAL CAREER COUPLE	THE EGALITARIAN COUPLE
HE is the breadwinner. SHE is the homemaker and child-raiser. HE competes and succeeds for both. SHE provides child care, and social maintenance for both.	HE is the breadwinner (with some involvement in family and home). SHE is the homemaker and child-raiser but she also works, usually for a specific purpose (such as better vacations for the family, extra home comforts, her own personal satisfaction). HE has the dominant career but acknowledges her contribution to their quality of life, and her need for some kind of outside activity. SHE works, but neither of them thinks of her as having a "career".	HE is committed to a professional career. SHE is committed to a professional career. The couple think of themselves as being a dual career family. BUT, one of them (almost always the woman) takes on more than 50 per cent of the responsibility for housekeeping and child-raising, and provides less than 50 per cent of the income.	HIS and HER roles vis-a-vis career and home are essentially the same. BOTH work; they have an equal commitment to their jobs. BOTH do 50 per cent of the housework. BOTH do 50 per cent of the child-raising.

Note: Couples often change their relationships on the spectrum. Perhaps the most typical example we see of this today is the couple who in their twenties assume a traditional couple role. In their thirties, after their children are in school, they shift to the semi-traditional role. And in their forties, after the children have left home, they become a dual career couple. In practice, however, at this stage, women typically may be a number of years behind men who have held full-time, uninterrupted careers.

Exercise 17: Pro's and con's of a dual career family

- Each partner makes a list of:

  A   The advantages of being part of a dual career family
  B   The disadvantages of being part of a dual career family.

- The lists are shared and discussed.

What are the implications for us of being a dual career family?

Overall, do we wish to be a dual career family?

DECISION 4. What career pattern do I want?

This has already been examined on page 85.

The decision-making process you need to follow is summarised in the following diagram.

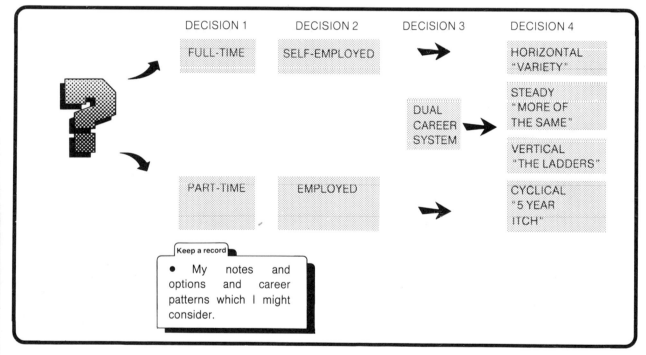

DECISION 1	DECISION 2	DECISION 3	DECISION 4
FULL-TIME	SELF-EMPLOYED	→	HORIZONTAL "VARIETY"
		DUAL CAREER SYSTEM →	STEADY "MORE OF THE SAME"
			VERTICAL "THE LADDERS"
PART-TIME	EMPLOYED	→	CYCLICAL "5 YEAR ITCH"

Keep a record

- My notes and options and career patterns which I might consider.

 FACT 1 in 4 recently retired people would be interested in returning to paid work.

11% of men aged 50–59 in 1987 and 8% of men aged 60–64 were not seeking work because they believed there was none available to them.

WHERE AM I?

What have you learned about the possibilities for your own career pattern?

....
....
....
....
....
....
....
....
....
....
....
....
....
....
....
....
....

Up until now you have been involved primarily in collecting data from yourself only on who and where you are. The final section of Question 2 will involve you getting data from other important people in your life.

Who are You? — What do others think?

To see ourselves as others see us is a vital element in RAINBOW BUILDING. We should not allow ourselves to be shaped by other people but we should open ourselves up to the possibility of learning from them.

A useful way of looking at oneself is through a window†, which demonstrates the different facets that contribute to that unique individual — ME!

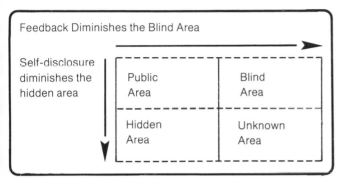

PUBLIC AREA: This refers to those aspects of ourselves that we know about and that we are comfortable for others to know about too.

BLIND AREA: Those parts of ourselves that others see but of which we remain in blissful ignorance.
This has been called the "bad breath area", but this only refers to negative aspects of ourselves. Often we are unaware of positive or interesting things that people think and feel about us because they have never told us and we have never asked them.

HIDDEN AREA: Our innermost thoughts and feelings, expressed to few or perhaps to no-one.

UNKNOWN AREA: This is sometimes called the area of potential growth . It refers to the potential we all possess that has not yet come to light.

Only by getting feedback from others can we discover more of the blind and unknown areas of ourselves.

Exercise 18: How do others see you?*

RAINBOW BUILDING SKILL: Knowing yourself
Research skills
Communicating

This exercise involves a process that you might wish to initiate to a greater or lesser extent.

†This model was developed by Joe Luft and Harry Ingrams and is commonly called the JO-HARI WINDOW.

You should have completed exercises on the following:

1. My lifeline

2. How do I spend my time?

3. My work and play values

4. Finding my transferable skills

5. What are my interests?

6. Choosing where to live

7. The ages of me

8. What life stage am I at now?

9. What kind of career pattern do I want?

You will undoubtedly obtain value from talking through your answers to these, and any of the other exercises, with friends and colleagues, but there are particular exercises where additional data can be invaluable. Here are some suggestions that have been carried out by participants on our workshops:

● Get a spouse or close friend to do the WORK VALUES card sort in terms of the values they see you demonstrating. From this you will learn which values they see you expressing as well as merely holding.

● Ask friends and colleagues to do the TRANSFERABLE SKILLS card sort according to how they see your skills.

● Ask colleagues and your bosses what skills they see you as owning. Ask them also what areas for development they see in you.

● Ask a spouse or friend to do the INTERESTS check according to what interests they see you as having.

In addition to these you might like to ask your spouse or partner to do the exercises on where they would like to live and work.

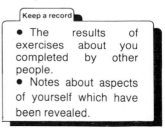

Keep a record
● The results of exercises about you completed by other people.
● Notes about aspects of yourself which have been revealed.

91

Rainbow Building Summary Sheet

WHERE AM I NOW?

I am at the following LIFESTAGE	The career pattern I want: (circle)
....	HORIZONTAL STEADY VERTICAL CYCLICAL
	DUAL CAREER
....	FULL-TIME PART-TIME
....	EMPLOYED SELF-EMPLOYED

I have learned the following about myself from other people?

....

....

....

....

On the basis of that I will...

....

....

....

....

You are now about midway through this career and life management programme. You have collected a great deal of data about yourself from yourself and from others. Reflect on the following and record your thoughts for your AHA! folder.

How do I feel about myself and who and where I am right now?

What changes would I like to make?

92

Reviewing Your Contract

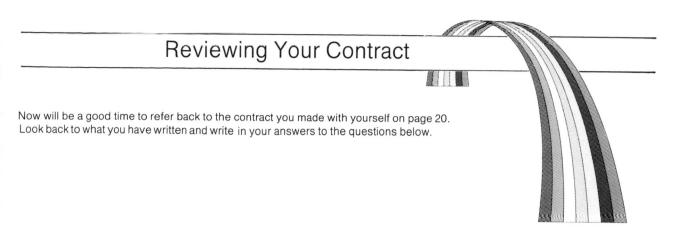

Now will be a good time to refer back to the contract you made with yourself on page 20. Look back to what you have written and write in your answers to the questions below.

What have I got so far from working with this book?

What have I been doing to get what I want?

Have I been sabotaging my efforts in any way?

How am I feeling about building my rainbows right now?

What else must I do to maximise my chances of getting what I want?

Am I committed to continuing with the process?

Question 3

HOW SATISFIED AM I WITH WHO & WHERE I AM?

Having thought about "who you are" in terms of your career and life so far, the next step is to reflect on the amount of satisfaction and dissatisfaction you are currently experiencing. Satisfactions can be clues to what is important to you and what you may want to preserve and retain. Dissatisfactions, on the other hand, are clues to what in your career or life may need remedying. This is not to say that you can achieve everything you desire, which is clearly not the case, as constraints — both internal and external — must limit everybody's range of choice. Frequently, however, we limit our thinking by focussing so directly on the constraints operating on us that we are able to achieve less than we might. In consequence, our careers or lives may not be as consciously shaped, chosen or satisfying as they might be.

The exercises in this section will help you to focus, in turn, on:
- your sources of satisfaction
- what you would like more, or less, of in either your present job, your career or your life
- objectives you may wish to set in order to achieve more of what you feel is important to you.

ROUTE MAP for "How satisfied am I with who and where I am?"

Assessing Your Use of Time and Satisfactions

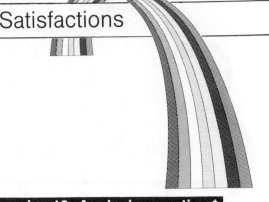

On page 24 you have already completed your TIME INVESTMENT RECORD and asked yourself questions about this. It is now time to begin to assess the level of satisfaction you are getting from that investment when compared with the time spent.

We find it useful to distinguish between MAINTENANCE, SOLD and DISCRETIONARY time.

- MAINTENANCE TIME – the amount of time spent maintaining yourself or others, cleaning, eating, tidying, shopping, cooking etc. Keeping things ticking over in your life.

- SOLD TIME – the time you 'sell' to an employer, an organisation or a customer, to produce income or some other reward. This concept is wider than simply the hours you spend 'doing' your job. It involves travelling-to-work time, follow-up time, etc.

- DISCRETIONARY TIME – the time you have free to choose exactly how you want to spend it. This may not always mean that you will enjoy what you choose to do. You may feel a responsibility to attend a local committee meeting, visit relatives, spend time learning about car maintenance because you cannot afford to pay for servicing, and you might not particularly enjoy any of them. It is your choice, however. It may not always feel like you have a choice, but you do.

THERE IS ALWAYS AN ALTERNATIVE

You may choose not to live with the consequences of an alternative, for example, being considered by your community as non-community minded, or facing criticism or your own guilt feelings for not visiting your relatives. But for every situation there are alternatives.

Sometimes the distinctions between these 3 elements of our time can be difficult to make. Everyday cooking is clearly a maintenance activity. If it is also a hobby of yours, you may spend much longer at it than you need to. In that case you are devoting some of your discretionary time to cooking too. These distinctions have to be subjective. Only you can decide under which of the 3 labels a particular activity comes.

Exercise 19: Analysing my time*

RAINBOW BUILDING SKILL: Learning from experience
Knowing yourself

Analysing your time

- Refer back to the Time Investment Record you made in Exercise 2.

- Use 3 differently coloured pencils/pens to colour in each section according to whether it is maintenance, sold or discretionary time.

- Now work through the Time Investment Record and make lists of your activities in each of the three categories using labels that make sense to you. Your lists might look something like the ones below:

Maintenance Time	Sold Time
Sleeping	At work
Eating	Travelling to work
Cleaning	Taking work home at weekends

Discretionary time

Time with my spouse
Walking, etc.

- Take a large sheet of paper. Write your lists down the left hand side and mark off in hours, a scale across the top to make a chart like the one shown overleaf. The divisions represent hours of time (you should try to get as many as possible across your sheet because 'sleeping' and 'at work' could take up to 60 of them!).

- Looking back at your Time Investment Record add up, as accurately as possible, the total time spent on each activity over the whole week. Mark off the bars on the chart to show the total using the same colours as before. When you have finished check how much of the bars you have coloured in – it should represent about 168 hours (the hours available to you in 1 week).

For example

Maintenance time	2	4	6	8	10	12	14	16	18	20
Sleeping										
Eating										
Cleaning										
Tidying										
Shopping										
etc.										
Sold time										
At work										
Travelling to work										
Work at home										
etc										
Discretionary time										
With spouse										
Walking										
etc										

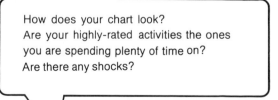

Watch Point

Beware of too broad categories. In the example above, "At work" would need to be broken down further and similarly "Time spent with my spouse" needs to be broken down into doing what and for how long.

Exercise 20: Analysing my satisfactions*

RAINBOW BUILDING SKILL: Learning from experience
                          Knowing yourself

- Work down your list again and make an assessment of how much satisfaction each activity gives you using the star system below.

✸	not at all satisfying
✸✸	
✸✸✸	
✸✸✸✸	
✸✸✸✸✸	extremely satisfying

- Write in your star rating next to each activity on the chart.

How does your chart look?
Are your highly-rated activities the ones
you are spending plenty of time on?
Are there any shocks?

- **Making changes**
  It's worth thinking about which of the activities you might like to do more of. Not all activities which are relatively satisfying give more satisfaction if you do a lot more of them – they may be better in small but regular doses.

Look at each of the activities to which you have given a 4 or 5-star rating. Think about which ones really would give you extra satisfaction if you could do more of them. Some will be easier to increase than others.

If you do want to do more of some activities, where will you find the time? You will have to reduce the time spent on some other activities. Which ones will you choose and how will you spread the cut-backs? Not all activities with a low star rating will be easy to cut, but start by looking at low-rated activities in your 'Discretionary' group...

Are there any activities which are missing
altogether from your busy life
you would like to include?

- **Other changes to think about**
  Look back at your notes about the balance of your life roles (Exercise 2) and see if they suggest any other changes you might want to make.

Were any of the roles missing
from your life?

Do you want to change the
balance of time spent in different roles?

- **Planning an ideal (but realistic) timetable**
  You may have decided you would like to increase or decrease the amounts of time spent on some activities, or you may have decided that increases are not necessary but that protection of certain time is. Start with types of activity you wish to increase or protect and make a set of decision statements like the one below.

I plan to spend at least _____ hours per week doing

Keep a record

- Your bar charts for time and satisfaction.

- Your ideal chart.

Exercise 21: My career and life brain pattern*

RAINBOW BUILDING SKILL: Knowing yourself

This exercise is designed to take a snapshot of your entire life as you experience it now. This will help you to draw up a list of your primary satisfactions and dissatisfactions. Some of you might prefer to do just that, but we wish to introduce you to a technique that many people find helpful in getting many related and unrelated thoughts on to paper in a short period of time. The technique is called brain patterns and was developed by Tony Buzan, initially to take notes when listening to lectures. The example below may initially look totally chaotic, but closer inspection will reveal the thinking 'flows' that occurred when the person produced this brainpattern.

The advantages of brain patterns over ordinary list-making are that:

● the main idea is more clearly defined;

● the relative importance of each idea is clearly indicated, as more important ideas will be nearer the centre and less important nearer the edge;

● new information is easily added;

● the links between ideas are easier to see.

You always begin a brainpattern in the centre of a large piece of paper with the key concept, in this case 'My life and my career'. See what comes into your head. Branch out from the centre. Name the branch line close to the centre. Take it as far as your mind wants to take it.

Print your words in capitals, the pattern will be easier to read later.

The printed words should be on lines and each line connected to other lines.

The example below will give you an idea of the process.

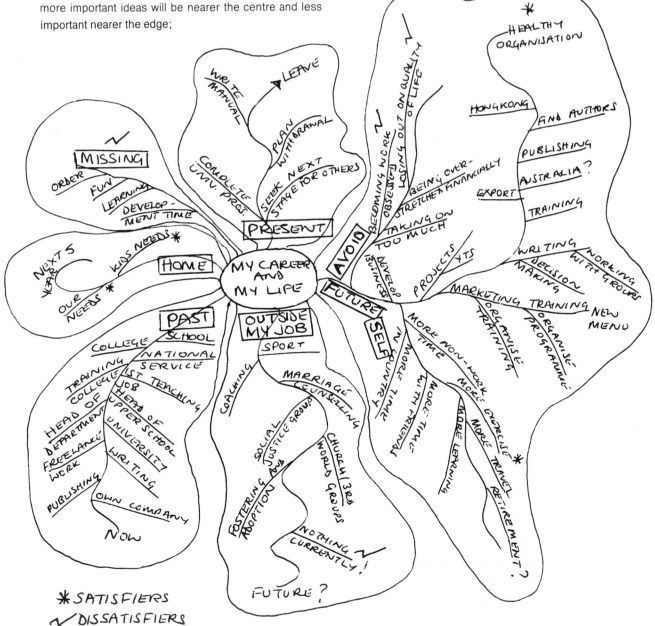

* SATISFIERS
✓ DISSATISFIERS

Do not worry about order or presentation as this will interrupt your thinking flow. In many cases you will find that this will take care of itself. Put everything you can think of around the central idea.

After you have finished see what links to what and connect them up.

You can always draw your pattern again if it will make it easier to understand.

Use different colours to distinguish between your primary branches, either by writing with different colours or by circling the branches with different colours.

Colours, shapes, symbols, arrows, etc, can be used.

- Use one colour to refer to conditions, aspects, ideas, etc, in your brainpattern that will denote 'satisfiers'. Circle any item that seems to be a 'satisfier' for you.

  List all your satisfiers on a separate sheet of paper. Each time one is mentioned, write it down, e.g.

  > family
  > job
  > friends
  > travel
  > community activities
  > learning/studying

- On the same sheet of paper write down the answers to the following questions by drawing the appropriate words from your list:

  > Who are the key people in my life and career?
  > What do I need from my paid or unpaid work?
  > What do I enjoy doing?
  > What surprised me in my list?

  > Is there anything missing? Would I have expected some satisfiers to be here which are not? Why aren't they on my brain pattern? Which of my satisfiers would I like more of?

- Now circle all the items on your brain pattern that are 'dissatisfiers' in some way. Use another colour for this. You might even find that some items classify both as satisfiers and dissatisfiers.

- List all your dissatisfiers on a separate sheet of paper as you did for the list of satisfiers.

- Write down your answers to the following questions:

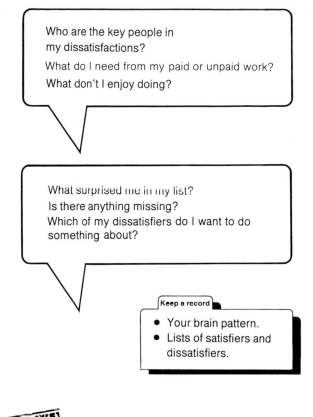

> Who are the key people in my dissatisfactions?
> What do I need from my paid or unpaid work?
> What don't I enjoy doing?

> What surprised me in my list?
> Is there anything missing?
> Which of my dissatisfiers do I want to do something about?

Keep a record
- Your brain pattern.
- Lists of satisfiers and dissatisfiers.

FACT 1 in 5 adults are retired. Retired people can expect to live another 15 years (men) and 20 years (women), that is, over 25% of one's adult life will be spent in retirement.

FACT

"Q   What has a workforce of 3 million, putting in 18 million hours a week, and an income of £5,000 million?
A   It has been nicknamed 'the white economy'. It is the voluntary sector."

Judy Kirby[14]

HOW SATISFIED AM I?

You have analysed in greater depth just what pay-offs you are getting from how you spend your time. You have delved into what really gives you satisfaction in your career and your life and explored the causes of your dissatisfaction. Participants on our workshops have found it useful to summarise these under the headings of People and Activities. However, if you have items that do not really fit this classification, ignore the classification. It is only an aid, and as with all the aids in this book, if it does not work for you – don't use it!

My major SATISFIERS are:

	People	Activities
IN MY JOB		
IN MY CAREER		
IN MY LIFE		

My major DISSATISFIERS are:

	People	Activities
IN MY JOB		
IN MY CAREER		
IN MY LIFE		

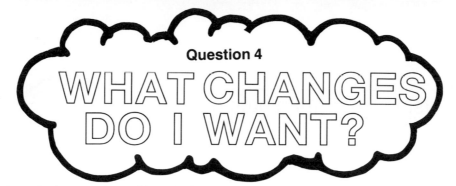

Question 4

WHAT CHANGES DO I WANT?

It is not our claim that everybody can attain or achieve absolutely everything – we do believe, however, that most of us rarely achieve all that we are capable of, largely because we do not become clear about what we want or would prefer to be doing. Until we do, we cannot even begin the journey towards our next stage of development through which we will realise more of our potential and achieve more of what is important to us.

ROUTE MAP for "What changes do I want?"

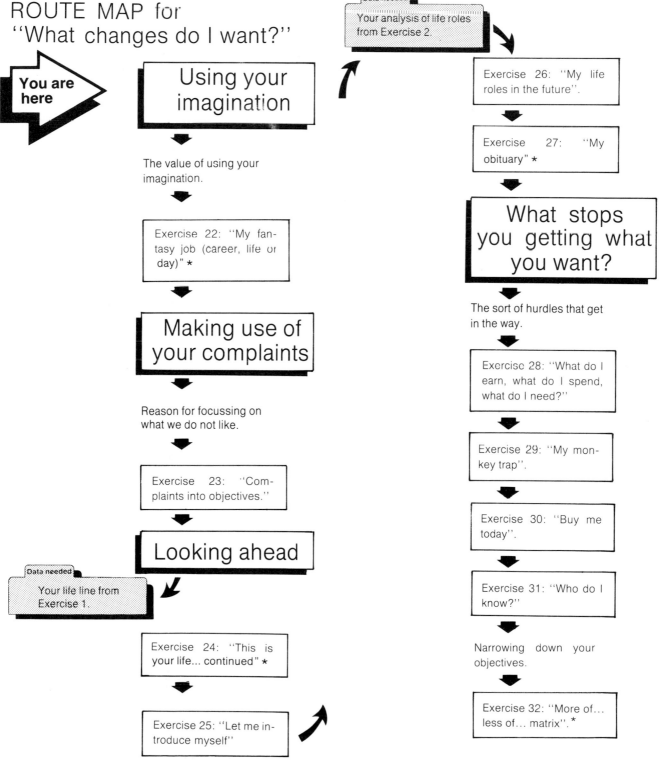

You are here

Using your imagination

The value of using your imagination.

Exercise 22: "My fantasy job (career, life or day)" *

Making use of your complaints

Reason for focussing on what we do not like.

Exercise 23: "Complaints into objectives."

Looking ahead

Data needed
Your life line from Exercise 1.

Exercise 24: "This is your life... continued" *

Exercise 25: "Let me introduce myself"

Data needed
Your analysis of life roles from Exercise 2.

Exercise 26: "My life roles in the future".

Exercise 27: "My obituary" *

What stops you getting what you want?

The sort of hurdles that get in the way.

Exercise 28: "What do I earn, what do I spend, what do I need?"

Exercise 29: "My monkey trap".

Exercise 30: "Buy me today".

Exercise 31: "Who do I know?"

Narrowing down your objectives.

Exercise 32: "More of... less of... matrix". *

101

Using Your Imagination

The first exercise in this section invites the use of what is for many an underused dimension of ourselves – our imagination. In our hard, practical, workaday world this speculative, potentially creative faculty is often regarded as largely escapist and detached from reality, and therefore of doubtful value. Those who spend too much time using their imagination are often labelled 'dreamers' or 'day-dreamers', which implies an element of time-wasting and is regarded largely as pointless. We would challenge this.

In using your imagination, or in a fantasy journey, what you can do is to get in touch with those possibilities which would be interesting, attractive or desirable for you. Such flights of fancy can provide clues as to where you would like to be, or what you might want to work towards – which, because it seems too impractical, you may have scarcely even bothered to think about. Using your imagination, thinking the unthinkable, dreaming the impossible, need not be a waste of time.

This kind of exercise will be easier for some personality styles than for others. The practical, logical person might respond less enthusiastically, inclining towards hard, researched, proven data and methods. The enthusiastic individual often takes more readily to the possibility. Whatever your inclination, however, we would suggest there are gains to be made from an excursion into the realm of fantasy. Have a go!

Exercise 22: My fantasy job (career, life or day)*

- You are to imagine for a time that there are no constraints for you of time, money, age, health, status, ties etc. This exercise asks you to remove all thoughts of constraints for the next few minutes – ignore them!

- Appreciating that there are no restrictions, select one of the following to work on. Begin with which ever seems easiest and put a ring around it:

  MY FANTASY JOB

  MY FANTASY CAREER

  MY FANTASY DAY

  MY FANTASY LIFE

- Think through your chosen topic in some detail and write down your version of what would be involved e.g. in your FANTASY JOB identify details such as, status, salary, job specification, style of work, the life-style which accompanies it, what you would actually do and not do, with whom you would work, in what kind of surroundings, with what kind of authority and responsibilities, with what kind of working day, week etc.

In your FANTASY CAREER go into the area of your career as a whole, commenting, for example, on how it might ideally develop from your present position. Include your preferences and wants in matters such as your career progression, status and income sought, pattern of employment and life-style desired, opportunities for using your present skills and developing others, integration of your career development with other life-roles, opportunities you hope will occur for you, etc.

Your FANTASY DAY is an invitation to log the events of what for you would be the 'perfect day'. Where would you be, what would you do, and with whom, if anybody? What time would the day start and end, would it include work, leisure, family and in what proportion etc?

Your FANTASY LIFE offers an opportunity to consider your ideal life as a whole. In this fantasy you can outline what would be your scenario for the perfect life. This picture could include how long you would like to live, the pattern of work, the integration of work, home and social life, status, income, life-style etc.

In short, whichever topic you choose, write in as much detail as you can so that the fantasy becomes a full picture rather than simply an outline. (Some people prefer to represent the details of their fantasy in picture form or through symbols rather than in written words – if you prefer to do it that way, please do. The fact remains that the more details you have, the more use the exercise is likely to be to you.).

- When you have written down your FANTASY, it is ready to be worked on. Think carefully through the following:

> What are my thoughts, feelings, reactions to doing the exercise?
> What does the fantasy indicate about what I would value, appreciate, aspire to, or want for myself?

What are the differences between my fantasy and my reality?

How much of my fantasy is achievable at present or might be in the future? If I can't have it all, can I have some of it?

"The danger of premature evaluation is that nothing will be conceived."

Roger von Oech

What are the barriers to my achieving some of my fantasy and how might these be overcome?

What would be the consequences of my working to achieve some of the features of my fantasy, for myself and for other people?

You see things as they are: and you ask "Why?"
But I dream things that never were: and I ask "Why not?"

G. B. Shaw

Would the pursuit of the features of my fantasy and their achievements be worth the possible consequences?

What objectives would I like to set myself on the basis of this exercise?

Make a note of any objectives you have identified and place these in your "Aha!" Folder.

Keep a record
- Your fantasy.
- Things you would need to change to achieve your fantasy.

Making Use of Your Complaints

Sometimes it is easier for us to focus on what we do not like in a particular situation than on what we do like. Irritants and dissatisfactions are often easy to identify because of the discomfort they cause – it is difficult to ignore things which actually hurt. But remember, pain has the purpose of alerting us to something which needs attention.

Our complaints and dissatisfactions can therefore be used positively. They bring to our notice something we would prefer to be different and they form the starting points from which to make changes – so that things will be more like we want them to be.

By being explicit about what we don't like we can discover more of what we do like. Complaints can be converted into objectives!

This exercise invites you to look at current complaints you may have about your job, career or life and to use them to begin to identify what you might work to change.

- CLARIFYING COMPLAINTS. Sometimes dissatisfactions are expressed in very general terms, e.g. I am not getting much out of my job at the moment – and this means they are difficult to translate into objectives. To help make your complaints specific, the exercise asks you to look at your job in more detail. If you choose to look at your life, your career, or just one day, you will probably need to add your own categories of sources of dissatisfaction.

  But, just for this example, our focus is on features of our jobs which commonly provide sources of dissatisfaction – if for you there are other sources, then simply add them to the left-hand column.

  In the 'COMPLAINTS' column of the chart note quite briefly any significant complaint you may have in a particular area – consider each area in turn e.g.

  PEOPLE/RELATIONSHIPS 'not enough contact with colleagues'.

Enter NIL in the areas about which you have no complaints.

- In the next column, note a specific example of your complaint. The more specific you can be, the more you will know what needs to be tackled. e.g.

  PEOPLE/RELATIONSHIPS 'No coffee break – we each take coffee in our own office'.

When you have completed all you wish to in the complaints and examples columns, ask yourself:

> How do I react to seeing what I have written?
> How great/small, constant/rare are the causes of my complaints?

> How much are the matters I complain about my responsibility or the responsibility of others?
> Are there complaints for which I can't provide examples? What does that suggest?

COMPLAINTS INTO OBJECTIVES†

Job	Complaints	Examples of Complaint	Objectives	Indication of Success
People/ Relationships	Not enough contact with colleagues	No coffee break – we each take coffee in our own offices	Organise a social area for coffee breaks	Room 203 set aside with comfortable chairs; coffee urn purchased
Finance				
Prospects				
Activities or tasks	etc.			
Time		etc.		
Surroundings			etc.	
Life-style				etc.
Other				

†This exercise was adapted from Loughary and Ripley[15].

The next stage in this exercise is to translate complaints into objectives. Your complaints are comments on 'how things are' at present. Now we would like you to begin to describe 'how I would like things to be'.

Take each complaint in turn and write in the objective column what you would like to do to improve things e.g.

PEOPLE/RELATIONSHIPS 'Not enough contact with colleagues'

OBJECTIVE To organise social area for coffee breaks (or to organise, with others, a staff social club).

Try to express each objective in positive terms. Refer to what it is that *you* want to do — setting objectives for somebody else can be very ineffective!

Be specific and include a definite time by which you hope to achieve your objective. Objectives stand more chance of becoming realities if:

You act positively

You take responsibility

You know specifically what you wish to achieve, and by when.

In the last column try to list an example of what would result if you achieved your objective — i.e. what will be a mark of success for you. (Thinking of a specific example can be a check of how realistic are your objectives — if the example looks very remote and unlikely then you may want to review your objectives.)

It is particularly useful to talk through your plans for turning COMPLAINTS into OBJECTIVES with another person. That can be really helpful, since it will:

● encourage you to explore and clarify your dissatisfactions and what you will do about them;

● offer the possibility of a 'contract for change' in which you openly declare your intentions (and are more likely, therefore, to be committed to achieving them);

● invite support for some of the things you wish to do.

Place any objectives you have as a result of this exercise in your 'Aha!' Folder.

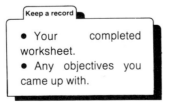

Keep a record
● Your completed worksheet.
● Any objectives you came up with.

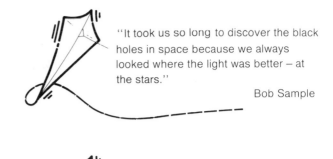

"It took us so long to discover the black holes in space because we always looked where the light was better — at the stars."

Bob Sample

"No one ever stumbled across anything sitting down."

Charles Kettering

WHAT CHANGES DO I WANT?

The last two exercises have provided a way of thinking (in an oblique way) about changes we would like.

> What have I learned about
> what I would like to change?

....

....

....

....

....

....

....

....

....

....

....

....

....

....

....

....

We continue with some more exercises designed to open up your thinking about what additional personal changes you might wish to make.

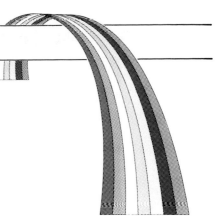

Exercise 24: This is your life... continued.*

- Return to the "Drawing my lifeline" exercise you completed on page 23. That exercise stopped at the point you have reached now. We want you to continue your lifeline

  – AS YOU WOULD WISH IT TO CONTINUE...

  Add as many details as you can of your life ahead as you would want it to be. Then reflect on these questions.

> Is this in any way different from how I think it *will* continue? In what ways?
>
> What might prevent me from getting the lifeline I want?

> Which constraints can I do something about and which do I think I could do little or nothing about?

> How many of the impediments stem from factors outside of my control, and how many might emanate from within myself? What can I do to get more of what matters to me?

Keep a record
- Your new lifeline.
- Notes.

Exercise 25: Let me introduce myself...

This is a verbal alternative to the last exercise, which in its own way can be equally challenging because we have to verbalise our thinking to another person.

- Find a colleague with whom you can do this exercise.

- First, take 10 minutes to introduce yourself to your friend as you are now. Having completed the section on WHO AM I? you should have plenty to talk about!

- Next, spend 5-10 minutes introducing yourself as the person you were exactly 10 years ago. This is more powerful if you speak in the first person – as if it really was you but ten years younger.

- Finally, spend 5-10 minutes introducing yourself as the person living the life you think is most likely ten years from now. Again, try to keep it in the first person.

> Which of these introductions did I find most difficult?
>
> Why?

> Is there a difference between what I hope my life will be like ten years from now and what I realistically think it will be like ten years from now?

> What are the implications of this for my future decision-making?

Keep a record
- Your notes about the way you described yourself in the future.

Exercise 26: My life roles in my future

On page 25 you completed an analysis of what proportion of time you are spending in your range of life roles.

- Imagine yourself as you think you are most likely to be ten years from now. Write down what you would see yourself being and doing for each life role.

....

....

....

....

....

....

....

Keep a record

- The completed list.

RAINBOW BUILDING SKILL: Knowing yourself
                          Learning from experience.

Newspapers publish obituaries which give a description of a person's life-history, achievements, key relationships, etc. plus an evaluation of the person's life.

● Write your obituary† as an objective journalist might do it, including the time and manner of your death. It should not be more than 500-600 words.

After you have completed your obituary ask yourself these questions:

> How might I have liked that obituary to read differently?
> What can I do now to ensure that my obituary will read like I would wish it to read?

> How would I summarise that person's life?
> Can I think of a fitting epitaph?
>
> Write it here.

....
....
....
....
....
....
....
....
....
....
....
....
....
....
....
....

†Some people have experienced difficulty and distress in completing his exercise, but eventually they have found it of great value.

WHAT CHANGES DO I WANT?

> What have I learned about the sort of future I would like for myself?

....

....

....

....

....

....

....

....

....

....

....

....

....

....

....

....

....

....

....

....

What Stops You From Getting What You Want?

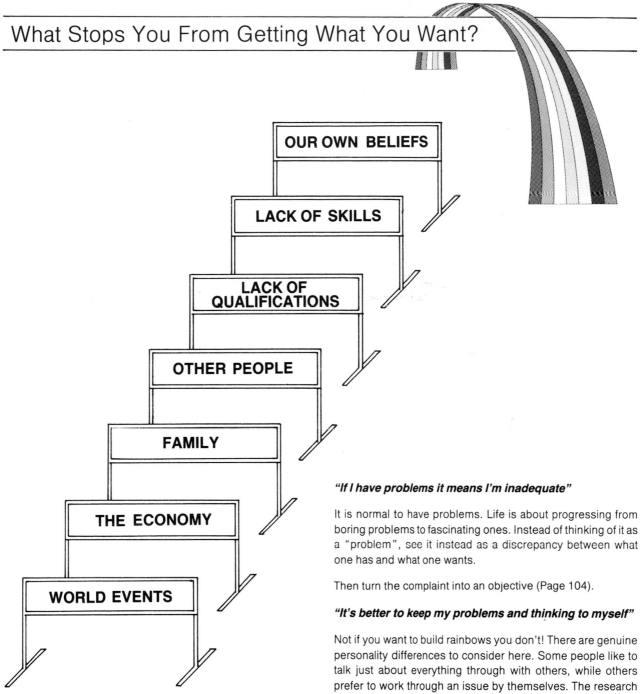

OUR OWN BELIEFS

LACK OF SKILLS

LACK OF QUALIFICATIONS

OTHER PEOPLE

FAMILY

THE ECONOMY

WORLD EVENTS

The hurdles designed to prevent us from getting what we want

Some of these hurdles are outside of our control, for example, world events and the economy; some are partially under our control, for example, the influence that we allow our family and other people to have over us, and lacking qualifications and skills; some are totally under our own control, namely, the beliefs that we have about ourselves and the attitudes we have developed.

Let us examine some of the beliefs that we have found can be blocks to RAINBOW BUILDING.

"If I have problems it means I'm inadequate"

It is normal to have problems. Life is about progressing from boring problems to fascinating ones. Instead of thinking of it as a "problem", see it instead as a discrepancy between what one has and what one wants.

Then turn the complaint into an objective (Page 104).

"It's better to keep my problems and thinking to myself"

Not if you want to build rainbows you don't! There are genuine personality differences to consider here. Some people like to talk just about everything through with others, while others prefer to work through an issue by themselves. The research findings on problem-solving, however, are very clear. The quality of problem-solving is almost always improved by involving other people's contributions.

There may be times when we need to be alone to sort things out, but any conclusion or decision will undoubtedly benefit from discussing it at some point with people who you know are useful resources and providers of feedback.

"I cannot live on less than I earn now".

In our experience this is hardly ever the case. What is required is a careful identification of present income and expenditure matched alongside priorities. Test this out for yourself with Exercise 28.

Exercise 28: What do I earn, what do I spend, what do I need?

don't think you must use this one as it stands. It may not fit for you. Feel free to design your own.

• Prepare a budget sheet for you or your family.

We reproduce an example of a typical budget sheet† but

BUDGET SHEET

INCOME	AMOUNT	OUTGOINGS		AMOUNT
Wages		Money	Savings	
Building society interest			Interest charges	
Child allowance			Rent/mortgage	
Any perks e.g. company car cheap house			Rates	
loan, etc.			Insurance	
		Car and other travel	(Re)payments	
other			Tax	
			Insurance	
			Fares: work	
			other	
			AA/RAC	
			Petrol, oil	
			Servicing, repairs	
		Food	All food	
			Meals out (inc. school)	
			Alcohol	
		Appliances	(Re)payments	
			TV Licence and rental	
			Servicing	
		Holidays	Travel	
			Accommodation	
			Other	
		Household expenses	Gas	
			Electricity	
			Phone	
			Cleaning materials	
			Cleaning, repairs	
			Other	
		Entertainment and leisure	Newspapers	
			Meals/shows	
			Sports	
			DIY materials	
			Garden	
			Subscriptions	
			Children's lessons	
			Other	
		Furnishing	Furniture	
			Soft Furnishings	
		Clothing	Clothes, shoes	
		Miscellaneous	Birthdays, Xmas	
			Tobacco	
			Life insurance	
			Hairdresser	
			Other	
			TOTAL	

†Adapted from *Consumer Decisions*, with permission from the Open University.

For this kind of analysis you can begin to determine what you absolutely must have to live, as opposed to what you would choose to have.

For example:

- you could sell your car and travel by bike and bus.

- you may need a house but could you sell your existing one for a profit and buy a cheaper one?

- you may need a holiday but how about a home-exchange plan, or self-catering instead of a hotel?

Before you say 'Well, that takes all the fun out of life!', remember, that we are looking here at what is absolutely necessary.

> What have I eliminated?
> Can I gain the satisfactions provided by those items elsewhere or in a cheaper way?

For example, stop eating out so much and experiment with a new cooking cuisine at home.

Buy fewer books and make more use of the public library.

> If I were starting up again just what would I need? (You can strip away the present accoutrements and expectations you have developed over the years). Do I really still need all the income that I have? What are the implications of this?

One conclusion from this could also be that this confirms for you that you have insufficient income. Your issue would then be to generate some alternatives to acquire extra income. (See Resources Section on page 148).

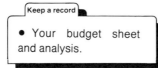
Keep a record

- Your budget sheet and analysis.

"I can't live without...   money
                              status
                              a particular person
                              my work
                              etc?"

Many of us trap ourselves into a lifestyle because of assumptions we make of what we must have before life is worthwhile. Our hunger can sometimes be so consuming that we pursue goals which clearly are not in our own best interests.

In some parts of the world where people enjoy monkey meat, they have developed a novel way of trapping monkeys. A coconut is hollowed out through a small hole in the shell. Boiled rice, which monkeys apparently adore, is placed inside the hole which is just big enough for an average sized monkey-fist to squeeze through. The shell is tied to a tree. Now, when the greedy monkey discovers the shell and the rice, he also discovers that he can just get his hand inside the shell, but as soon as he takes a handful of rice, he cannot get his hand out again! The monkey, you might predict would drop the rice to escape. But instead he cannot bring himself to let go and sits watching the hunters come closer and closer until they club him to death. Most of us have our own monkey traps: things, ideas, people that we cannot let go of even if it means our stultifying and perhaps dying, psychologically and even physically (e.g. with stress-related diseases). We must have material possessions, or security of job, or the permanence of a relationship at all costs, or a belief of how the world should be as opposed to how it is. Looked at this way, perhaps it is easier to understand just how a monkey can be so stupid!

Exercise 29: My monkey trap

RAINBOW BUILDING SKILL: Knowing yourself

- Thinking through the story of the monkey trap, write down an equivalent trap in your life.

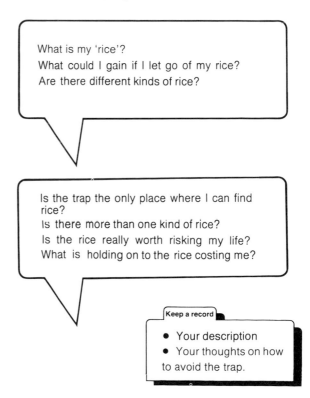

> What is my 'rice'?
> What could I gain if I let go of my rice?
> Are there different kinds of rice?

> Is the trap the only place where I can find rice?
> Is there more than one kind of rice?
> Is the rice really worth risking my life?
> What is holding on to the rice costing me?

Keep a record

- Your description
- Your thoughts on how to avoid the trap.

"It is undignified to have to promote or sell oneself"

This relates to a huge myth, namely, that talents will always be spotted. Our experiences suggest that talents first have to be put on show.

Why should anyone have confidence in you unless you give them some evidence for it? Exercise 30 will invite you to do this.

Of course, you cannot provide that evidence unless you have it. That is why your answers to Question 1: WHO AM I? are so crucial.

"Somewhere in the world there is THE JOB waiting for me"

From Section 1 you should have discovered that for your interests, skills and values there will be many jobs that you could do and would probably be very happy doing.

In the UK alone there are 23 million jobs and 3,000 occupational titles.

To a large extent, too, a job is what you can make of it. Jobs are not like ready-to-wear clothes that you have to fit yourself into. While there will always be limits to the pattern, to a certain extent you can always cut some of your own cloth.

"The job I have now is ideal and therefore it always will be"

We have already discussed the rapid rate of technological change which means that in the unlikely event of you staying exactly the same the chances of your job staying the same (or even just staying), are minimal.

Just as new needs develop as old needs are satisfied (see page 48) for our lives in general, so is the case with jobs.

An American research study[6] has shown that a person's needs from a job change over time. To begin with job security and safety is vital – just making sure that you are seen to be competent enough to hold the job down. Next comes the need to be accepted and to have one's work recognised. During these stages, too much autonomy and challenge may actually prevent you from performing at your best. These factors assume greater importance only after your more basic needs are met.

The same research showed clearly that after 15 years or so, even the most enriching job tends to becoming boring.

The message for us here is that we must periodically review what we are getting out of our jobs, and that we should not get angry with ourselves or worry if we become dissatisfied with what we nave previously found satisfying. That is what life is about. It is called DEVELOPMENT.

"What ever I do or plan is useless. It will all eventually be determined by... my firm... my family... the Government"

There will always be factors out of our control, but many things are open to our influence. In the final analysis we always have control over our own reactions to any event or decision. We can create unnecessary frustration by assuming that we can or should be able to influence everything.

You cannot change the world but you might be able to change your bit of it.

"Somewhere in the world there is THE PERSONNEL MANAGER, FIRM or BOSS who will discover me and my potential"

How? Not unless we make ourselves known, communicate our skills and qualities and market ourselves as a desirable product. If we can't be bothered to advertise ourselves, why should anyone else be interested enough to do it for us?

Exercise 30: Buy me today

- Imagine yourself to be a product. Your task is to launch this new product successfully.

To sell any product successfully you need to believe in it. To believe in it you need to know just what it is capable of, but also any deficiencies or problems there might be with it, because you, as the sales person, will be held accountable.

The table overleaf gives an example filled in by one of our participants.

We would like you to produce:
- a 'product analysis' on yourself,
- an assessment of your development needs,
- an appropriate sales slogan, if you were to promote yourself as a 'product',
- a rationale explaining why somebody should buy a 'product' like you.

Summarise the ASSETS
of this product

Skills

"Can drive, type, organise,
write, research, communicate
well"

Personal Qualities

"Enthusiasm
Determination
Conscientious"

Values

"Reliable
Honest
Hard-working"

Other

"Willing to share skills
Looks younger than age"

Summarise any possible
PROBLEM AREAS

Skills

"Can over organise instead of
getting on and doing things,
poor number skills"

Personal Qualities

"Easily distracted
Can be over jolly"

Values

"Needs to be appreciated
A bit 'goody-goody'"

Other

"Tendency to flare-up
Doesn't bother about her
appearance"

What FURTHER DEVELOPMENT is required for this product?

"This product needs better packaging and more drive to do really well. It is rather conventional and ordinary at the moment but could be marketed as a jolly fun package for special occasions."

• Create a sales slogan that typifies this product and simultaneously presents it in a favourable light.

....

Examples from participants

"Get it done and have some fun – Anne's the one".
"This is a no nonsense practical product with no gimmicks".
"Will work cheerfully to achieve any job undertaken".

In no more than 50 words say why you would buy this product.

I would buy this because ....

....

....

....

Keep a record
• Your product specifi-cation.
• An advert for yourself.

"It's unethical to think of people in terms of how helpful they might be to my career"

Using people as resources is not the same as "using" people in some manipulative way especially if we are also open to be used as resources by others.

People are invaluable for information, for support and sometimes for advice. Armed with specific questions you can learn more about a job or a leisure pursuit in 30-60 minutes from a well-informed person than from spending 6 hours in a library.

One of the most valuable things you can do in searching out job opportunities and leisure options is to 'plug' yourself in to networks of people.

We so often fail to ask for help from the human resources that are all around us and at our disposal.

 Only 12% of jobs in the UK are found through jobcentres.

 Nearly 60% of new jobs are filled as a result of people hearing about them from friends or as a result of a direct approach to an employer.

Exercise 31: Who do I know?

RAINBOW BUILDING SKILL: Research skills.

• List the names of relatives, your friends, your colleagues (Check your address book). These need not be people who are immediately obvious as useful contacts. List the names for their purpose may only become apparent later.

You will probably have at least 100 names by now. This is your PERSONAL CONTACT NETWORK.

Yet each of these people has a PERSONAL CONTACT NETWORK of their own, which gives you access to 5-10,000 people even allowing for overlap between networks.

• Begin to analyse your own network.

What jobs are represented?

What interests?

What skills?

What special knowledge?

Keep a record
• Your network.

Narrowing down your objectives

Exercise 32: More of... Less of... Matrix*

RAINBOW BUILDING SKILL: Objective setting

This matrix is one that many participants on our workshops have found to be useful for collecting together all the possible areas for personal change that the rainbow building process has identified thus far. If you find that it inhibits you rather than facilitates you, don't use it. You will need to find an alternative way of collecting up your personal data to enable you to decide which areas of your life require some action.

- Using the following Matrix identify in each category what you would like more of, or less of, in terms of contact with particular PEOPLE or in terms of the things you spend time on, ACTIVITIES. (The central column, 'Keep the Same', can be used to register what is satisfactory at present and you may find it useful to enter details in that section also.) The more specific you can be in your entries the more useful they are likely to be at the next stage. Produce your own matrix on a large sheet of paper if this one is not large enough. Examples of the entries might be:

		MORE OF	KEEP THE SAME	LESS OF
Present Job	People	Contact with colleagues doing similar work.	The amount of contact time with clients (as distinct from staff)	Staff bringing issues for me to confirm decisions they have already taken
	Activities	Creative forward planning new ideas sessions	Amount of responsibility and supervision of others work	Routine paper work

		MORE OF	KEEP THE SAME	LESS OF
Your Present Job	People			
	Activities			
Your Career	People			
	Activities			
Your Life in General	People			
	Activities			

- Circle the 3 things you would most like to do something about right now.

WHAT CHANGES DO I WANT?

What have I learned from my FANTASIES about what changes I want in my life?

From my LIFE REVIEW and MY LIFE CHOICES exercises I know that I want to change...

What OBJECTIVES do I have arising from my COMPLAINTS?

What stops me from getting what I want?

Do I want to do anything about it, and if so, what?

What is my own ADVERTISING SLOGAN?

What 3 things do I want MORE OF or LESS OF?

Question 5

HOW DO I MAKE THEM HAPPEN?

The key to getting more of what you want, to making things more like you want them to be, is likely to be the precision with which you can SET OBJECTIVES and MAKE ACTION PLANS. Failure to achieve much of what we would like in life can be traced to one or all of the following:

- low motivation,
- unclear objectives,
- ill-formed action plans.

We are assuming that, like all RAINBOW BUILDERS, you will be motivated to work for what you want, so we would now like you to give attention to clarifying your objectives and identifying the steps you will take to achieve them.

ROUTE MAP for "How do I make them happen?"

Setting Objectives

An objective is a desired outcome, target or result. It states what you want to achieve, e.g.

'I want to get a job which involves less stress and gives me more free time".

Objectives are important in defining what we want, in giving us a sense of direction, in offering us a chance to shape our own development.

"IF YOU DON'T KNOW WHERE YOU ARE GOING YOU WILL PROBABLY END UP SOMEWHERE ELSE!"

An objective states simply what we want to achieve, it does not describe tasks or activities which we will undertake to achieve it – those will be part of your ACTION PLAN to achieve your objectives. For example:

"I will buy a selection of newspapers to look for job vacancies", is part of an action plan.

Exercise 33: 12 steps towards clear objectives*

RAINBOW BUILDING SKILL: Objective setting and
Action planning
Making decisions

- Refer back to your MORE OF... LESS OF MATRIX, or whatever summary sheet you have used.

- Write down on separate pieces of paper each of the 3 objectives you wish to do something about.

- For each objective take the following steps. Write down your answers. At the end of this process you should have defined at least 3 clear objectives.

1. State your objective clearly – start with the word "To..." followed by an action word. For example: "To work for promotion to Head of Department in my present job."

2. Ask yourself whether there is an objective behind your objective. Ask why you want what you want – there may be other ways of getting it, for example: if you are pursuing responsibility, status, or extra money there may be other ways of achieving it without actually being promoted.

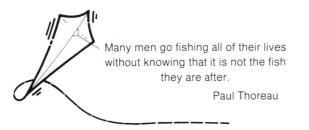

Many men go fishing all of their lives without knowing that it is not the fish they are after.

Paul Thoreau

3. State clearly how you will know when your objective has been reached – this will ensure that your objective is clear.

4. Make your objective as specific as possible, for example, not "I want my life to be more rewarding"... but, "I want to get more satisfaction from my job by replacing some of the paperwork with time to do creative forward planning".

5. State when you want to achieve this by, and why you choose that date. For example; "I want to achieve promotion by this time next year, because to wait longer would be frustrating".

6. Be clear for whom you want this. If it is not for yourself, will the other person find the objective acceptable? Is this relevant?

7. Check whether any of your objectives conflict. For example, if you have said that you want to work for promotion to Head of Department but also that you want to spend more time with your family, then you have to decide whether these two objectives are compatible. If any of your objectives conflict then you will obviously have to identify which ones have priority and work on those.

8. Identify any constraints (external or internal) which will make your objective more difficult to achieve.

9. Identify any resources (external or internal) which will assist the achievement of your objective.

10. Check that your objective is realistic – as before, talking it through with someone else (or with several other people) can provide useful alternative perspectives on how to tackle it.

11. Ask whether there is anything to stop you achieving your objective now. If not, you are ready to start. But if there are obstacles, then obviously you have as an initial objective to work to overcome those particular constraints.

12. How do you feel about what you have just decided to do? You may need someone who will give you real support while you work on achieving your objective.

This process can be repeated for any number of objectives.

Keep a record
- State your 3 objectives.

Exercise 34: Force-field analysis

RAINBOW BUILDING SKILL: Making decisions
Objective setting
and Action planning.

Force-field analysis is a way of improving your changes of achieving an objective or an action plan. It can be a method for examining what is involved in changes we may be thinking of making, and of identifying which forces may be helpful in making the changes, or which may work against the changes.

The method was developed by Kurt Lewin to demonstrate efficient and inefficient ways of achieving personal change.

In any situation where we wish to make a change there will always be some forces at work assisting us and some forces at work resisting us.

For example:

Emma and Bill live in London. They both have good, well paid jobs. They have always talked of moving to the country, away from the city and nearer to Emma's parents who are getting older. Bill is not happy in his present job and had found a business close to where her parents live which he wants them to take on together. Emma, however, has excellent career prospects and does not want to give up now. How then does Bill attempt to create conditions which will render Emma more open to change? A typical approach is to extol the virtues of the new scheme, the chance of living in the country, of getting away from the rat-race of the city and near enough to her parents to visit more often. However, using this approach is more likely to increase resistance to any move than to inspire Emma to join him.

The following diagram represents the forces working for and against Emma's acceptance of this move.

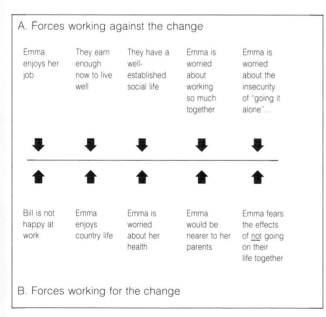

A. Forces working against the change

| Emma enjoys her job | They earn enough now to live well | They have a well-established social life | Emma is worried about working so much together | Emma is worried about the insecurity of "going it alone"... |

| Bill is not happy at work | Emma enjoys country life | Emma is worried about her health | Emma would be nearer to her parents | Emma fears the effects of not going on their life together |

B. Forces working for the change

The approaches that Bill has tried have all been concerned with reinforcing the upward pressures, namely emphasising the beneficial effects a move could have for him, their lifestyle and her parents.

However, our model is something of a physical one, and every physicist knows that if the forces operating on an object in a state of equilibrium are increased in one direction, then the forces in the opposite direction must increase equally if the equilibrium is to be maintained. This means that our arrows now look like this:

A

B

What has happened is that forces operating on each side are now significantly stronger, and tension is at a higher level.

Emma's frustration will increase, and her resistance is likely to harden.

What happens if Bill uses the other alternative open to him and concentrates on the downward forces (A) that make Emma resistant to change? This approach is called reducing resistance. If Bill tackles her concerns about the scheme and succeeds in reducing her resistance, then a new equilibrium is reached, but at a lower level of tension.

This is like stopping a car by taking one's foot off the accelerator, without using the brake.

A

B

The following exercise invites you to use this approach, alongside the more traditional one of building on the forces working for change.

The technique is to:

1. Identify your objective.

    ● State what you want to achieve, very specifically using the word "To...", and include when you hope to achieve it (i.e. "by...")

    ● Make sure you have stated only one objective. Deal with them one at a time!

2. List the forces working IN FAVOUR of what you want to achieve

    ● A positive force is anything which will contribute to your achieving your objective.

- When listing forces, be very specific (i.e. what, who, where, when, how much, how many, etc) Remember these forces may be inside or outside you.
- Indicate how the force will contribute to your achieving what you want.

3. List all the forces working AGAINST what you want to achieve.

   - Again, be specific.
   - List all factors, inside or outside yourself which will work against you.
   - Indicate what effect each force is likely to have on your achieving your objective.

4. Analyse the forces.

   - Identify which forces are most important, (these will be real, not assumed, and will have a significant effect on whether or not you can achieve your objective).

   - Circle all the important forces on your list.

   - Obtain any additional information you feel you may lack about any important force.

5. Weaken the negative – strengthen the positive.

   - Work on each important force in turn.
   - Identify ways in which you can reduce, minimise or eliminate (not exterminate!) each force working against you. Indicate any that you really cannot find a way of reducing by writing "no action possible" against it.
   - Identify ways in which you can increase, strengthen, or maximise each positive force. Work on one at a time.

6. Assess how feasible your objective or action plan seems to be.

   Ask yourself: Do the positives clearly outweigh the negatives or will they when I have maximised and minimised them?
   - If the answer is "yes", ask yourself again "Do I really want to achieve this?"
   - If the answer again is "yes", adopt your objective and begin to work on these forces.
   - If the answer is "no", then your choice is to abandon it or change it. For example, it may be possible to modify the original by reducing your sights or revising the target time.

If You Are Presented With Options

Exercise 35: Cost benefit analysis

It can be useful in helping us to choose between different options to see represented the COSTS and the BENEFITS of each option.

- Write down the options you wish to consider, for example:

  to wait for promotion in my present job.

  to seek a more senior job in a similar department in another company.

  to seek to transfer to another department in my present company and change my direction.

- Write the first option at the top of a sheet of paper. Divide the page down the middle and head the column on the left COSTS and the one on the right BENEFITS. (see diagram below). Enter in the COSTS column any disadvantages you (or you and others) can think of if you were to pursue that option. When you have finished listing all the COSTS you can think of, read back through the list. Attempt to grade each cost on a 1 to 10 scale as an indication of how you feel about the prospect e.g. 1 if you think it is a very slight disadvantage, 10 if it feels to be a major disadvantage to you. Score the rest in between.

  Finally, put a circle round the two biggest disadvantages.

Cost Benefit Analysis (example sheet)

OPTION: Waiting for promotion

COSTS	RATING	BENEFITS	RATING
No change of scene	2	I know the job and can do it well	(7)
No change of people	5	Little stress	3
Lack of challenge	8	The company knows my strengths	3
May wait in vain	8	I need not move house	(8)
Feeling helpless	(9)		
Someone else might beat me to it	(9)		

- Move now to the BENEFITS column under your first option and list any gains you might make from choosing that option. Grade the benefits on a 1 to 10 scale as an indication of how much a gain you feel it would be e.g. 1 if it feels only slightly advantageous, 10 if it feels to be highly advantageous to you. Score the rest in between. Finally put a circle round the two most attractive advantages from your point of view.

  Repeat this process for each option!

- Place your cost/benefit balance sheets alongside each other.

- Examine, think about or talk through your reactions to looking at each sheet again.

- Ask yourself, or identify, whether any option seems on balance to give you most of what you want.

- If it does, decide whether the costs of it are acceptable to you. If so, begin to make it happen!

- If there is no option which is clearly better for you than another then you have to choose either (a) to postpone the decision or (b) risk choosing one option when there is no convincing indicator.

- Write down, or declare what you have decided.

NB It can be useful sometimes to think through "What happens if I do nothing, or fail to make a decision?" – sometimes the consequences of inertia are not considered!

Keep a record
- The results of your cost-benefit analysis.

123

Rainbow Building Progress Check

HOW DO I MAKE THEM HAPPEN?

Using the techniques outlined collect together all your objectives and make them as clear as possible. Look back through your AHA! Folder.

Action Planning

When you have a clearly defined OBJECTIVE the next step is to develop an ACTION PLAN.

An ACTION PLAN provides you with the answer to the question:

"What do I do to achieve my objective?"

The steps in ACTION PLANNING are as follows:

1. Have a clearly defined objective.

   Too many action plans fail because the objective is not clear enough in the first place.

2. Start with what YOU are going to do NOW.

   The following diagram graphically portrays how action plans can get lost in the swamp, if you try to change too much or plan too far ahead.

3. Be very specific about the steps you will take to achieve your objective.

   For example, not, "I'll have a chat with my boss".. but, "I will try to see my boss on Thursday to discuss my current

job performance and ask about ways in which I might get promotion".

4. Arrange the action steps in a logical flow laid out so that even a computer could understand it!

5. Be aware that one action step will often involve you in planning a prior one. For example:
   "I will telephone the boss's secretary this afternoon to arrange an appointment for Thursday morning".

6. Decide when you will review your progress and write this into your action plan.

7. Transfer your plan to a diary to remind you of the particular dates by which the steps need to have been completed.

Contracting with others is particularly useful to ensure that you are sticking to an action plan.

8. Always be prepared to change the plan as circumstances change or if some of your steps do not turn out as you have wished.

Exercise 36: My action plan*

RAINBOW BUILDING SKILL: Objective setting and Action planning.

Take one of your objectives and develop an ACTION PLAN for

it. My objective is: ....

....

....

....

....

....

....

....

....

What I need to do is:
List the most useful action steps without worrying about their sequence.

....

....

....

....

....

....

....

....

....

....

....

Number them according to which comes first.

I am going to start with Step 1 on .... (give date)

I am going to start with Step 2 on .... (give date)

I will review my progress on .... (give date)

I should know whether my objective has been reached or not by .... (give date)

GOOD LUCK! AND DON'T GET LOST IN THE SWAMP

You can now return to your other objectives and produce action plans for them.

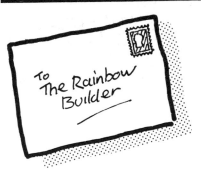

Keep a record
- Your example of an action plan.

Exercise 37: A letter to myself*

Not to be opened until (a date six months ahead).

....

A particularly effective method of reviewing progress is, at this stage, to write a letter to yourself. Give the letter to someone who could be relied upon to post it to you exactly six months to the day after you have written it. By then you will, most likely, have forgotten all about it. Its appearance on your doormat can generate feelings ranging from delight to despair as you see just how far you have achieved, or moved towards achieving, your objectives.

- Spell out clearly what you hope to have achieved in the six months after writing the letter for each of your priority objectives.

One alternative would be to send yourself a photocopy of the summary sheet for this question. We, personally, always prefer the informality of a letter!

Rainbow Building Summary Sheet

HOW DO I MAKE THEM HAPPEN?

My major OBJECTIVES are: (in order of priority)	To be achieved by:	ACTION PLAN? (tick if you have one)

Question 6

WHAT IF IT DOESN'T WORK OUT?

We suggested earlier that as you worked through the first five questions there might be times when it would be appropriate to turn to Question 6. As you worked through the exercises you may have felt frustration over the constraints in your life which restrict your options or make the changes you want to bring about more difficult. Perhaps you felt disappointment over past opportunities missed. Even if you did find the exercises stimulating and constructive you will still need the lifeskills of coping when things don't work out for use in the rest of your life.

ROUTE MAP For: "What if it doesn't work out?"

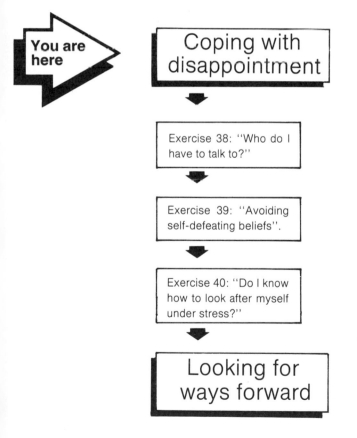

You are here

Coping with disappointment

Exercise 38: "Who do I have to talk to?"

Exercise 39: "Avoiding self-defeating beliefs".

Exercise 40: "Do I know how to look after myself under stress?"

Looking for ways forward

Coping With Disappointment

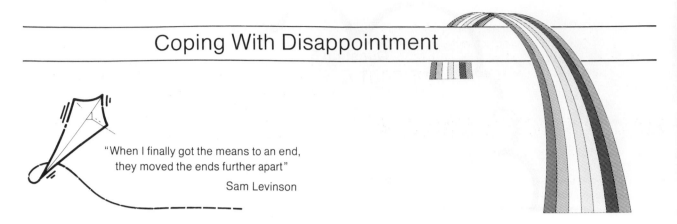

"When I finally got the means to an end,
they moved the ends further apart"

Sam Levinson

However clear our objectives and specific our action plans, however much time and energy we invest, there are always some factors outside our control which could result in our not getting what we want.

In addition, we do make mistakes! Our aims might not be realistic, our skills insufficiently developed, or we may even change our minds!

Taking the risk of succeeding requires us also to take the risk of failing. The alternative would seem to be to sit tight and let life happen to us. That way we can stay out of the rain-storm but we won't have a chance to build a rainbow.

Although we can, through successful career and life management, keep our disappointments to a minimum we cannot expect all of our plans and projects to succeed. And when a disappointment does occur it can be inappropriate to tell someone, "We can learn more from our mistakes than from our successes". When our plans do not work out we need to sound off about our feelings of disappointment, frustration and anger. Yet, most people do discover in the long run that they can learn a great deal by looking back and analysing what went wrong and considering alternative steps they could have taken or recognising the skills they lacked at the time.

It is helpful to acknowledge that not all of our plans will work out and to have suitable strategies ready for coping at these times.

We avoid using the word failure because too many people apply the word to themselves rather than to their plans. It can be helpful to recognise "Yes, this particular plan of mine failed", but it's extremely self destructive to think "I am a failure because my plan didn't work out"!

When you reach a point at which you realise things are not working out you need to consider two questions:

- How can I cope with the disappointment?
- What else can I try?

When a plan doesn't work out there are two areas a RAINBOW BUILDER has to manage.

EMOTIONAL and RATIONAL

The alternative strategies we suggest later are all very well if you are feeling strong and rational but that is often the last thing you feel when you have to face a major disappointment.

The emotional reactions, for most people, will have to be dealt with first.

> How do you feel when faced with great disappointment?

- Think back to a particular disappointment in your life. It may help to write down the details.

- Recall your first reactions – how did you feel? – what did you feel like doing?

- To what extent were these the typical feelings you have in response to disappointments?

- Now think about what you actually do at these times. List the typical things that you do when you face disappointment.

Coping with disappointment will usually involve one or a combination of:

- Getting rid of bad feelings.

- Having someone to talk to.

- Talking constructively to yourself.

- Looking after yourself under stress.

Look back at your responses above. Which of these four did you use?

1. ***Getting rid of bad feelings.*** Crying, shouting, beating a cushion, digging the garden, going for a run or a swim, playing squash, are all common ways in which people do this. Keeping these feelings inside you or worse still not being able to admit to yourself that disappointment generates bad feelings all add to the building up of stress and make the disappointment more difficult to cope with.

130

Now that you've thought about it a bit more, do the ways you typically cope with disappointment allow you to get rid of the bad feelings? Which of these suggestions might you try another time? Can you think of others that might particularly suit you?

Exercise 38: Who do I have to talk to?*

RAINBOW BUILDING SKILL: Looking After Yourself

• Write in the names of people you know who provide you with these different kinds of support in your job and away from your job.

2. ***Having someone to talk to.***

A problem for many of us is that we often expect most of our support and emotional sustenance from one or two people. We sometimes act as if it is wholly reasonable to expect to get all of our needs satisfied by a single person – usually a spouse, or one's immediate family, or by one or two close friends. The following exercise will help you to identify just who is in your support network whilst making the point that support is a many-faceted thing. You do have a choice to extend it, plug gaps, make changes.

MY SUPPORT NETWORK

TYPES OF SUPPORT	AT MY JOB	AWAY FROM MY JOB
Someone I can always rely on.		
Someone I just enjoy chatting to.		
Someone with whom I can discuss the exercises in this book.		
Someone who makes me feel competent and valued.		
Someone who gives me constructive feedback.		
Someone who is always a valuable source of information.		
Someone who will challenge me to sit up and take a good look at myself.		
Someone I can depend upon in a crisis.		
Someone I can feel close to – a friend or intimate.		
Someone I can share bad news with.		
Someone I can share good news and good feelings with.		
Someone who introduces me to new ideas, new interests, new people.		

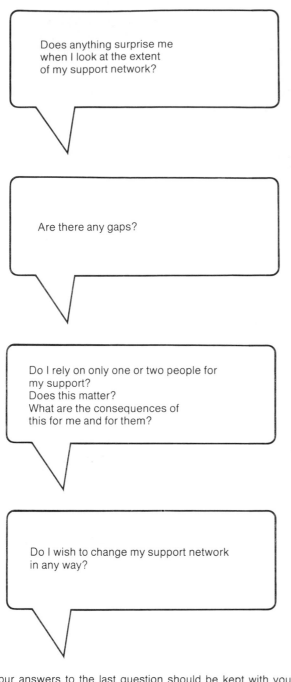

Does anything surprise me when I look at the extent of my support network?

Are there any gaps?

Do I rely on only one or two people for my support?
Does this matter?
What are the consequences of this for me and for them?

Do I wish to change my support network in any way?

way process: they willingly give support and hope to receive it when they need it.

Some people feel it's important to keep their problems to themselves and manage on their own so as not to bother other people. But since most people like to be asked for help when it's really needed such an attitude could be seen as either misplaced pride or as a signal that the person, underneath his pride, feels he is not worth bothering about or doesn't deserve help.

If you find it difficult to identify people to whom you could turn, go back to the 'Personal Contact Network' you drew up in Exercise 31 and check through to find those, not in your immediate close circle of friends, who could offer appropriate support if you asked them.

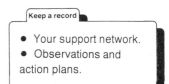

Keep a record

- Your support network.
- Observations and action plans.

It's always possible that because of the nature of the problem, or because you are away from home or have moved that you may not be able to think of anyone who could help. In this case a local Citizens Advice Bureau can suggest sources of voluntary or professional help.

Remember too that the Samaritans (any telephone operator will give you the local number) advertise that they offer a 'Listening ear' service around the clock. They also know where else you might seek help. You may be most unlikely ever to need this type of help but knowing that it exists and how to make use of it is a valuable lifeskill and would ensure that you would know how to cope if the occasion did arise.

Your answers to the last question should be kept with your previous work on Question 3: 'What changes do I want?' in your AHA! FOLDER.

It is sometimes difficult to feel that you can ask for support.

However most people are happy to offer this kind of support. It helps, too, if you make a practice of seeking support rather than bottling things up. Then you will not find it so difficult to approach people when you do have to cope with major disappointments. For most people offering support is a two-

3. *Talking constructively to yourself.*

We will spend some time examining this skill because it is so crucial to us when things do not turn out well for us. The way we think is likely to have a highly significant influence on the way we feel and what we do. The way in which we perceive a given situation, what we "Tell ourselves" as we think about it, will have a decisive effect on what feelings we experience and on our actions which follow as a consequence.

Typically when some unfortunate event or experience happens to us we feel bad. We assume that our bad feelings are created by that event; i.e.

$$EVENT \rightarrow BAD \ FEELINGS$$

What actually happens, however, is that something comes between the EVENT and the FEELINGS which will determine just what kind of feelings we experience. That 'something' we call SELF-TALK. This determines how we experience any EVENT, which in turn will determine what we FEEL and ultimately our ACTIONS.

The real sequence, therefore, is:

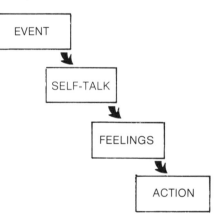

For example: This was one person's reaction to having failed a driving test.

EVENT:	This person's objective was to pass his driving test and he failed.
SELF-TALK:	"I'm pathetic. Anyone can pass a driving test. I'm a failure. I'm not risking being made to look stupid again."
FEELINGS:	He felt ashamed, frustrated, pathetic.

This is how it can affect, in turn, the fourth factor in our equation:

ACTIONS:	He felt so anxious not to experience those feelings again, he was determined not to put himself at risk. He was not going to try again.

All of this stems from assuming that your FEELINGS are caused directly by the EVENT, whereas they are determined almost totally by how you talk to yourself and interpret the event.

Before the FEELINGS stage the person above could substitute the following SELF-TALK:

"I am disappointed. It would have been good to have passed, especially as I practised so hard. However, things don't always turn out as we wish. I have failed but that doesn't make me a failure. I have to see what I can learn from my mistakes so that next time I won't make them again."

Look back to what you said you did when facing disappointment (p.130). Did you use negative self-talk then? If so, what might you have said that would be more positive?

It is important, therefore, in terms of looking after ourselves to realise that:

- What we think will decide what we feel and what we do.

- If we can exercise more control over what we think we can manage our feelings and our behaviour more effectively.

- If we do this we can take greater charge of ourselves and the situations we meet.

Realising this, is the first step to beginning to learn the kind of 'Self-talk' which will promote looking after ourselves and will reduce the likelihood of our being 'victims' of bad feelings or of situations we cannot control.

Exercise 39: Avoiding self-defeating beliefs

RAINBOW BUILDING SKILL: Communicating

Contrary to what we often believe, other people or things do not make us unhappy. We make ourselves unhappy by what we tell ourselves. We need to train ourselves to avoid negative or destructive self-talk and particularly to avoid thoughts which are based on self-defeating beliefs. These beliefs set up expectations in us of ourselves, of other people, or of the world, which are unrealistic and invite disappointment.

These beliefs lead to most of the feelings of worry, anger, fear, jealousy, depression and guilt that people experience. If we believe them we will think in terms of 'Things should be ....' or, 'People ought to be ....' and we will get angry or disappointed a great deal of the time when events or people do not live up to our expectations. If we can begin to accept that there are no 'Shoulds' and 'Oughts' and begin to think in terms of 'It would be preferable if......', or 'I may need to work to bring that about', then we will be more likely to act to make things more like we want them to be.

Overleaf is a list of some of the beliefs which are likely to produce problems, if our thinking is based on them. As you read the list circle the number in front of any to which you always or sometimes subscribe to.

1. I must be loved or liked by everyone, people should love me.

2. I must be perfect in all I do.

3. All the people with whom I work or live must be perfect.

4. I can have little control over what happens to me.

5. It is easier to avoid facing difficulties than to deal with them.

6. Disagreement and conflict are a disaster and must be avoided at all costs.

7. People, including me, do not change.

8. Some people are always good, others are always bad.

9. The world should be perfect and it is terrible and unbearable that it is not.

10. People are fragile and need to be protected from 'The truth'.

11. Other people exist to make us happy and we cannot be happy unless they do so.

12. Crises are invariably and entirely destructive and no good can come from them.

13. Somewhere there is the perfect job, the perfect 'solution', the perfect partner, etc, and all we need to do is search for them.

14. We should not have problems. If we do it indicates we are incompetent.

15. There is only one way of seeing any situation, i.e. the 'True' way.

- Remember the last time you felt bad about something — angry, jealous, resentful, etc. What were you telling yourself? Were any of these 15 beliefs the basis for your self-talk?

- Now, you are going to challenge the destructive self-talk that caused you those difficulties. Fill in the rest of the table for the event you have just thought about. Write down your self-destructive talk in your own words. They may well include condemnation of yourself and be full of what people should or ought to do.

The event:

___

What I felt:

___

What I was telling myself:

___

What it made me do:

___

What my self-defeating belief was:

- Now challenge that self-talk, re-interpret it by exchanging the shoulds and oughts for preferences. Talk to yourself about what you can learn from the experience. Tell yourself that you can behave differently next time.

- Fill in the table below with alternative constructive self-talk and the consequences that could have resulted:

Constructive
Self-talk

___

Feelings
Would be

___

Actions
Could be

If we can:

1. **avoid self-defeating thinking when difficulties arise;**

2. **develop ways of thinking (using self-talk) based on a more rational approach in time of difficulty;**

we will be more likely to manage ourselves and the situation more effectively when things do not turn out as we would wish.

"Men feel disturbed not by things, but by the views which they take of them"   Epictetus, 1st Century AD

There may be times when self-defeating talk becomes almost obsessional: you can't get such thoughts out of your mind. Here you have to try something that might sound silly but works – tell yourself firmly to "Stop" whenever you catch yourself doing it. Don't make it worse by saying to yourself "You are stupid to think like that". That's just more self-defeating talk. Just "Stop" and then move on to positive self-talk. Have some positive thoughts or pictures ready to put into your head automatically.

You can work steadily towards giving up all your self-defeating beliefs.

When you are under extra stress you may find that your favourites – usually the ones that allow you to say rotten things to yourself about yourself – creep back into your mind. This could be a sign to you that you need to pay more attention to looking after yourself under stress.

4.   *Looking after yourself under stress.*

Research has consistently shown that the fitter we are the more energy we have to cope with the problems that arise and disappointments that are inevitable in everyday life. Keeping fit will help us to prevent undue stress when things do not go well for us. Also when we do experience the ill effects of stress, physical exercise can help us to feel better.

We can dissipate stress through a fitness programme, dancing, sex – altogether if we're creative!

The other side to looking after ourselves physically is to learn to relax when all about us is movement, turmoil, frustration, and disappointment. There are many ways of relaxing and perhaps it appears strange to read of this as a skill.

The time to relax is when you don't have time for it!

We would certainly not wish to prescribe to people how they should relax but it is important for everyone to discover the techniques that work for them. We do regularly meet people who seem totally incapable of relaxing. Below are some techniques for relaxation.

Techniques which work directly on our bodies

- meditation
- progressive relaxation
- deep breathing
- yoga
- massage

Techniques which work indirectly through a psychological process

- listening to music
- reading a book, watching TV
- having a drink
- going to a peaceful place
- being with people we can be ourselves with

Stimulation as a way of relaxation

Sometimes when we feel tired we often do not feel like doing anything. Hard work can make us tired so that we physically need a rest. However, when high stress makes us feel tired a change to a stimulating activity can make us feel better and full of energy again. It helps to think about what is behind our tiredness. You could try the effect of:

- a brisk walk
- a quick shower rather than a relaxing soak in the bath
- dancing to a record
- phoning up a friend
- making a snap decision to go out somewhere (meal, film, bowling, bingo, roller skating – something different!).

Which of the options in this list have you tried?
Do they work for you?
Which others might you try?

Keep a record
- Your list of self-defeating beliefs, and what you can do to counter these.

Exercise 40: Do I know how to look after myself under stress?

RAINBOW BUILDING SKILL: Looking after yourself

When our plans (even the half-conscious ones) do not work out, we can easily feel under a considerable amount of stress as a result. Below are listed a variety of questions about 'Looking after yourself' in stressful situations.

Tick the statements to which you can answer 'Yes'.

( )　　Do I get regular exercise, or have a personal fitness programme?

( )　　Do I eat regularly and have a balanced diet?

( )　　Do I keep to a regular schedule?

( )　　Do I know how to say 'No' to things I don't want, and conversely, do I know how to ask for what I do want?

( )　　Do I give myself a break, or some kind of a 'treat' when under stress?

( )　　Do I have people to whom I can turn for help?
　　　　Do I actually turn to them?

( )　　Do I know how to relax?

( )　　Do I talk constructively to myself?

If you scored 7-8 you should be able to cope well with disappointment.

If you scored 4-6 you can cope with some disappointment but would benefit by developing your 'Looking after yourself' skills.

If you scored 0-3 you are likely to be incapacitated by disappointment unless you make definite plans to acquire better 'Looking after yourself' skills.

Space does not permit us to discuss each of these issues here, instead, look at the resources section on page 148 which refers to a number of available materials which are broadly concerned with 'looking after yourself'. Most of these should be available in your local library, or at least they could obtain copies for you. In addition to books, you could enrol in classes on 'Looking after yourself', or yoga, meditation, relaxation, massage, assertiveness, fitness, and time management. Your local library, newspaper, Citizens Advice Bureau, Adult Education Centre or College of Further Education are good places to find out what is going on in your area.

Looking For Ways Forward

When we have coped effectively with our feelings of disappointment, we are free to use our skills of RATIONAL THINKING to help work out what to do next.

If things do not work out as you wish:

1. Reappraise your action plan.

2. If that does not work, reappraise your original objectives.

3. Ask why it didn't work – what was due to your influence, and what was due to external influences?

4. Ask yourself what you can learn from the experience.

5. Always have a back-up plan (Plan B). Develop it alongside Plan A and try to identify check points during Plan A at which you can review progress and if necessary cut your losses and switch to Plan B. Your original plan should be flexible enough for you to be able to revise and improve it as you go along and to enable you to switch to Plan B if need be.

    By all means put everything you've got in to achieving Plan A but don't let the chance to reach your goal fall through because you haven't taken the time to consider other ways of reaching it.

6. Take a lateral step. Consider a different goal if your first choice proves unobtainable.

Whenever you are in a situation that you wish to change there are always four basic strategies for managing that situation – illustrated in the figure below.

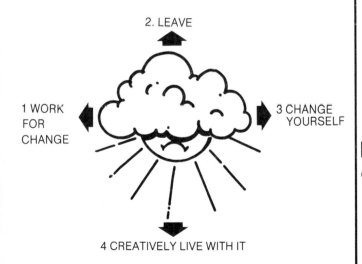

Strategy 1: Change the situation

The first strategy is often that of trying to change the situation to make it more like you want it to be. However, having tried to make changes to no avail, you are left with the other three options.

Strategy 2: Leave

You exit from the situation, job, relationship or problem.

Strategy 3: Change yourself

Perhaps if you changed your ambitions, attitude, behaviour, lifestyle etc., your situation would improve.

Strategy 4: Creatively live with it

This means much more than simply, "Putting up with it". It requires a conscious strategy so that you can minimise the undesirable aspects of the situation and maximise the desirable ones. Examples might include investing more energy in activities outside of your job (if dissatisfied at work), isolating yourself in a project in such a way that it reduces your contact with troublesome elements, or spending more time doing the things you enjoy and cutting down on the others.

Below is an example worked out by someone who was extremely dissatisfied with her job.

CHANGE THE SITUATION	LEAVE
Options	Options
• suggest a new project • negotiate for a re-definition of my job • suggest that meetings are more structured • ask for salary increase • arrange to work more with people I like	• get new job • get leave of absence • get industrial sabbatical • take early retire-ment • get transfer to another site
CHANGE YOURSELF	**LIVING WITH IT**
Options	Options
• lower my expectations • get retrained • undertake inservice training	• focus more on other areas of my life • go part-time • take a second job • take an Open University course

We have felt it necessary in this section to prepare you for the worst. Things won't always work out, you will make mistakes, others will block your goals. The challenge for you is how well you react to that?

Will you learn from the experience or disappear into the swamp underneath it?

WHAT IF IT DOESN'T WORK OUT?

1. List the techniques you use to deal with disappointment.

    Add new ones you are going to try.

    Physical: ....
    ....
    ....
    ....
    ....
    ....
    ....

    Psychological: ....
    ....
    ....
    ....
    ....
    ....
    ....

    List the key people in your support network: ....
    ....
    ....
    ....
    ....
    ....
    ....

2. Which 'Looking after yourself' skills do you need to improve or acquire?

    What are the next steps you have to take in order to do this?

    a ....   a ....

    b ....   b ....

    c ....   c ....

3. List your most common self-defeating beliefs.

    Translate each of them into more positive self-talk.

    a ....   a ....

    b ....   b ....

    c ....   c ....

AT THE END OF YOUR RAINBOW

ROUTE MAP for "The end of your rainbow"

You are here

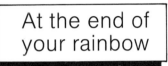

At the end of your rainbow

What have you gained?
Skills developed
Insights
Reminding yourself of what you have achieved
Conflicting or changing goals
A rainbow-building tool kit
Monitoring progress
When to use the exercises again
Alternative uses
Marriage
Consumer and political action

Dear rainbow builder...

Moving on

Resources

We have reached the end of our RAINBOW BUILDING programme. How useful has it been for you? This book offers you the chance to find out about yourself. It can tell you how to do it but only you can do the hard work involved. Return to the contract you made with us on page 20. How well have you stuck to the contract?

In part 4 of the contract you were asked to identify ways you have sabotaged yourself in the past. Did you catch yourself doing it this time? Are you now more aware of the ways in which you do it?

For example did you:

- Skim through the book meaning to come back and actually do the exercises – but didn't?

- Only start reading when you were too tired?

- Never allocate sufficient time to do enough work on it?

- Defeat yourself by negative self-talk and turn every exercise into an opportunity to put yourself down?

- Use any of this above list of devices to avoid acknowledging that it can be quite scary to explore yourself in this way?

We are not in a position to challenge you on this: but we are asking you to challenge yourself.

What have you gained?

You can review what you have achieved by looking through the notes you have made and at the progress checks and summary sheets.

Sum up what has proved most important for you in each of these three areas:

1. Information (facts) I've learned.

....
....
....
....
....
....
....
....
....
....
....
....
....
....
....
....
....
....
....
....

2. Skills I've developed.

....
....
....
....
....
....
....
....
....
....
....
....
....
....
....
....

3. Insights I've gained (Look through your 'AHA' folder).

....
....
....
....
....
....
....
....
....
....
....
....
....
....
....
....
....
....

Skills developed

At the start of this book we said a rainbow-builder needs to develop seven types of skills (page 11). The whole range has been covered but *knowing yourself* has been the main focus of the exercise. As a rainbow-builder you need to have a thorough understanding of your raw materials.

The table overleaf sums up which skills the various exercises have been helping you to build.

Which of the exercises have proved most useful for you? Put a tick in the skills columns on the next page opposite the exercises to indicate in which way you found each exercise to be helpful.

Now consider:

- Are there some exercises you left out that you would like to go back to?

- Do you wish to repeat some of the exercises?

- Which of the seven skills do you want to build up? 'Moving On', page 146, suggests how you could pursue this.

Exercise Numbers	Knowing yourself	Research skills	Learning from your experience	Communicating	Making decisions	Setting objectives making action plans	Looking after yourself
1. Drawing my life line.							
2. How do I spend my time?							
3-9 Clarifying my values.							
10. Finding my transferable skills.							
11. What are my interests?							
12. Choosing where to live.							
13. The ages of me.							
14. What life stages am I at now?							
15-17 What kind of career pattern?							
18. How do others see you?							
19. Analysing my time.							
20. Analysing my satisfaction.							
21. My career and life brain pattern.							
22. My fantasy job/career/life/day.							
23. Complaints into objectives.							
24. This is your life... continued.							
25. Let me introduce myself.							
26. My life roles in the future.							
27. My obituary.							
28. What do I earn, what do I spend, what do I need?							
29. My monkey trap.							
30. Buy me today.							
31. Who do I know?							
32. More of... less of...							
33. 12 steps towards clear objectives.							
34. Force field analysis.							
35. Cost benefit analysis.							
36. My action plan.							
37. A letter to myself.							
38. Who do I have to talk to?							
39. Avoiding self-defeating beliefs.							
40. Do I know how to look after myself under stress?							

Insights

In the future these may be your most vivid memories of working through this book. Insights are usually gained when we are thinking most deeply about ourselves – it's almost as if we have dredged them up. However it sometimes seems as if we find them too painful – or challenging, and they sink down again out of sight. We forget the insights we have gained.

You can help prevent this happening and gain most from them by taking each of the key insights you have just listed (page 140) and writing some action notes for them. Will you now be on the alert for certain situations to which you will try to react differently? Do you want to change yourself in any way? Or perhaps acknowledge and accept the person you now see yourself to be?

Reminding yourself of what you have achieved

Working through this book should have proved challenging and stimulating. It may at times have been hard work or painful. It's quite an achievement to have examined your life in this way. You should feel proud of yourself. Praise yourself – it's better than praise from others! You might like to write yourself a post-card noting exactly what you are proud of having done. You could pin it up picture side out where you can see it regularly. It will remind you of what's on the other side.

Conflicting or changing goals?

The Rainbow Building Summary Sheet you completed at the end of Question 5 may well have identified for you, that some of your goals conflict. Or you may realise that pursuing some of your goals would conflict with the goals of those you live or work with. This will probably mean that you need to reconsider the priority you give to the various values you have already looked at. You may also need to move on to consider what your values are for personal relationships, and for involvement and responsibilities within the community and society.

You've probably already found that at different times in your life you have chosen or been forced to give priority to different goals. It may well be the same in the future.

Your action plans will need to take this into account. Try making short-term and medium-term action plans:

1. Short-term – What will you achieve during the next six months?

2. Medium-term – What, at this moment, do you hope to achieve during the next five years? If you review this plan every year you will have a rolling five year plan that can be more responsive to the changing priorities you may need to give to your goals.

An additional strategy is to keep an up-dated list of what you hope to achieve before the end of your life. The list will certainly change as the balance of your values shift at successive life stages: Doing this can spur you on to make life happen, rather than to let life happen to you. With this list there is, however, a danger that you will suddenly flip from thinking, 'There's plenty of time to fit everything in', to, 'Good heavens time is running out'. If this happens you'll probably then recognise that it

counts as a 'mid-life turning point' and that you should go through this Life Management Review again.

A Rainbow-building tool kit

The skills you have learned *are transferable*. You *can* go on building rainbows.

Monitoring progress

You may decide to repeat some of these exercises either regularly or at certain times, especially if major changes are coming up. They can be used as a way of quality control monitoring for your life. On the next page are some suggestions as to how you might use them.

Exercise	When to use
Exercise 2 How do I spend my time? plus Exercise 19 and 20.	○ Regular review: demands and needs will vary. ○ When you are under pressure. ○ When you feel increasingly tired. ○ When you are having trouble meeting new commitments.
Exercises 7, 8 and 9 Values and needs	○ At different life stages (see Exercise 14) when priorities are likely to change. ○ When certain life events challenge your values.
Exercise 10 Transferable skills	○ Keep this updated (particularly if you want to keep an up-to-date curriculum vitae, but also as a morale-booster).
Exercise 11 What are my interests?	○ Check occasionally — your energies and enthusiasms may vary. ○ Do it to challenge yourself to try new things and to check if those you are saving up for later in life ever get done.
Exercises 14 Life stages	○ Check every five years.
Exercise 17 A dual career family	○ Do this when relevant.
Exercise 18 How do others see you?	○ Occasionally — if you begin to suspect that your image of yourself needs adjustment in the light of feedback from other people.
Exercise 21 My life and career brain pattern	○ Use to monitor changes in your 'satisfiers' and 'dissatisfiers'.
Exercise 26 Life roles in the future	○ Check in ten years time to see if you were right!

Exercise	When to use
Exercise 31 Who do I know?	○ Review and revise – this will alert you to where you are losing contact with parts of your network. Do you want to lose contact? Are you adding new people?
Exercise 32 More of... less of...	○ Monitor progress and make new action plans periodically.
Exercise 37 A letter to myself	○ Remember to open it!
Exercise 38 Who do I have to talk to?	○ Monitor regularly to see that you do. ○ Check when under stress since these are the people who can best support you.
Exercise 40 Do I know how to look after myself under stress?	○ This needs to be kept up all your life. Six monthly reviews will help.

You could make a note in your diary to check through this list during the last days of December when you are getting yourself together to face a New Year.

Alternative uses

The exercises have been developed to help you look at life and career management but you can adapt them to other issues that you want to examine or projects that you want to plan.

Many of them can be used at transition times when you are facing major changes in your life. You may have chosen to make the change and enjoy doing it but the knock-on effects of the change on the whole of your life and perhaps on to other peoples make it a stressful time.

Here are some ideas for just two other areas of life:

Marriage

• Exercises 1 and 24 can be adapted to explore the history and possible future of your marriage. Both partners should draw their own future life lines and discuss them with one another.

• Exercise 6 'Use of leisure' and Exercise 2 plus Exercises 19 and 20 'Analysing the use of time' may help both partners negotiate new contracts. So will Exercise 32 'More of..... Less of.....'.

• Exercise 17 'A dual career' needs to be done before marriage as well as at various stages during the marriage.

- Exercise 22 'Fantasy' – think about your fantasy partner and fantasy marriage. What does this tell you about yourself? What would be appropriate for you to share with your partner?

Consumer and political action

- Exercise 23 'Turning complaints into objectives' is probably the starting point.

- Exercise 33 'Twelve steps to clear objectives', Exercise 34 'Force field analysis' and Exercise 36 'my action plan' will help you develop a campaign.

- Exercise 35 'Cost benefit analysis' can help you see pros and cons of a proposed action or choose between options.

- Exercise 31 'Who do I know?' When members of a group pool the relevant parts of their networks supportive and influential people can usually be found.

"To go faster you must slow down."
John Brummer

Dear Rainbow Builder...

Before you move on, please accept this award
with our congratulations for completing this programme!

With these skills you will go far!

Moving On

This programme can be hard work. We would suggest that before you move on you relax, take a break, go and have some fun. Then come back and think about your plans for the future. Here are some suggestions you might try.

Your plans might include:

- seeking out more information;

- building up your life skills;

- gaining more insights into yourself.

Which areas?

Here are a few you might choose from:

- Further work/career management

- Personal relationships

- Looking after yourself

- Leisure interests

- Management skills

- Unpaid work options

- Planning for early retirement.

Resources

Your choice may depend on whether you want to concentrate on information, skills or insights. Consider which of these you might want to use:

Books

In general they are good for information. 'How-to-do-it' books for skills. 'How-to-do-it' human psychology books for insights as well as skills. Ask your library for help in getting relevant book lists.

Counselling/Advice

Ask at library or Citizens Advice Bureau for what's available in your area.

Consider using career counsellors, marriage counsellors — who accept any life-review concern as a suitable reason for seeking help, or psychotheraphy (ask G.P. for what is available on N.H.S. or privately).

Support/Interest groups

These self-help groups may be part of a national network or just a local initiative. C.A.B. and libraries should know about them. They may be information, support or action focussed.

Local classes

You may need direct personal tuition for learning certain skills. Being able to share your experiences with others is an additional benefit. Check local newspapers, libraries and Colleges of Further Education, Adult Education Centres and Community Colleges.

"People travel to wonder at the height of mountains, at the huge waves of the sea, at the long courses of rivers, at the vast compass of the ocean, at the circular motion of the stars; and they pass by themselves without wondering."
St Augustine

REFERENCES

1. Hopson, B. and Scally, M. *Lifeskills Teaching,* Maidenhead, McGraw Hill, 1981.

2. Hopson, B. and Scally, M. *Rainbows, A Teaching Programme for Career and Life Management,* Sheffield, COIC, 1991.

3. Sheehy, G. *Pathfinders,* London, Sidgwick and Jackson, 1983.

4. Figler, H. *The Complete Job Search Handbook,* New York, Holt Rinehart Winston, 1979.

5. James, Clive *Unreliable Memoirs,* London, Picador, 1981.

6. Campbell, D. *If You Don't Know Where You're Going, You'll Probably End Up Somewhere Else,* Niles, Illinois, Argus, 1974.

7. Kelly, E. L. "Consistency of the adult personality", *American Psychologist,* 1955, 10, 654-681.

8. Spender, D. *Invisible Women: The Schooling Scandal,* London, Writers and Readers Publishing Co-operative, 1982.

9. Holland, J. L. *Making Vocational Choices: A Theory of Careers,* Englewood Cliffs, N. J. Prentice-Hall, 1973.

10. Levinson, D. J., Darrow, C. N., Klein, E. B., Levinson, M. H. and McKee, B. *The Seasons of a Man's Life,* New York, Alfred Knopf, 1978.

11. Neugarten, B. L. "Adaptation and the life cycle", in N. K. Schlossberg and A. D. Entine (Eds), *Counselling Adults,* Monterey, California, Brooks/Cole, 1977.

12. Hopson, B. and Scally, M. "Changes and development in adult life: implications for helpers", *British Journal of Guidance and Counselling,* 1980, 8; 2.

13. Sperry, L., Mickleson, D. J., Hunsaker, P. L. *You Can Make It Happen,* Reading, Mass., Addison-Wesley, 1977.

14. Kirby, J. *Work After Work,* London, Quiller Press, 1984.

15. Loughary, J., and Ripley, T. *This Isn't Quite What I Had In Mind,* Eugene, Oregon, United Learning, 1974.

RESORCES

BOOKS AND MATERIALS

FOR CAREER AND LIFE MANAGEMENT

What Colour is Your Parachute? Richard Bolles, Ten Speed Press, 1988. This is a UK edition of the best-selling US guide to self analysis and "proactive" job hunting. The British supplement primarily consists of books and addresses and the US text is reproduced in its entirety. This makes the information component of the book less relevant to the UK which is a pity because the system is well-tried.

The Best Is Yet To Come: A workbook for the middle years, Maggie Smith, Lifeskills Communications, 1989. Shows how people can use the experience of early retirement as an opportunity to review their lives, learn to manage change, develop new interests, relationships and lines of work.

Lifeskills New Open Learning Workbooks, Barrie Hopson & Mike Scally, Lifeskills Communications 1991. 11 booklets in an easy to use, open learning format. Suitable for both individual and group use. Topics covered: Transitions, Communication, Assertiveness, Time Management, Manage Disappointment, Relationships, The Benefits of Balance, Creative Problem Solving, Creative Decision Making, Stress, Health & Your Lifestyle, Learn to Learn.

These booklets have been designed to follow the Code of Practice on Quality Open Learning (MSC 1987).

Manage Your Own Career, Dave Francis, Fontana, 1985.

Super Job Search, Peter K. Studner, Mercury, 1989.

FOR LIVING IN THE INFORMATION ERA

The Third Wave, Alvin Toffler, Pan, 1981. Crucial for an understanding of how the Information Era is fundamentally different from the Industrial Era. Very American, very stimulating, with a global perspective.

The Aquarian Conspiracy: Personal and Social Transformation in the 1980's, Marilyn Ferguson, Paladin 1982. A wide-ranging account of a unique change in values and relationships identified by the author as happening throughout the world.

Megatrends, John Naisbitt, Futura, 1984. The trends for the Information Era identified by a fascinating technique of trend analysis through local newspapers.

The Awakening Earth: Our Next Evolutionary Leap, Peter Russell, Ark, 1984. A highly stimulating, mind expanding survey of where human consciousness may be heading next.

The Age of Unreason, Charles Handy, Hutchinson, 1989. A Vision of an era of new discoveries, new enlightenment and new freedoms. An examination of the concept of discontinuous change and how it can be turned to advantage.

The New Realities, Peter Drucker, Mandarin, 1990. A changing analysis of the information-based organisation, the input of knowledge workers on organisations and the economy, and much more.

FOR ADULTHOOD AND SELF-DEVELOPMENT

Passages: Predictable Crises of Adult Life. Gail Sheehy, Bantam Books, 1982. Best seller which charts the progress of adults through all the key life stages. Fascinating case studies enable you to play "spot yourself".

Pathfinders: How to achieve happiness by conquering life's crises. Gail Sheehy, Bantam Books, 1983. An investigation of how satisfied with their lives American men and women are at different periods of the life cycle. It also gives great encouragement to people to take risks in their lives as that seems to correlate highly with reported satisfaction.

Spirit of Survival, Gail Sheehy, Bantam, 1987.

FOR WOMEN

Returners, National Advisory Centre on Careers for Women, revised edition 1990.

The Female Resource: An overview, Women in Management, 1989. A summary of facts and statistics about women in the UK.

Harnessing the Female Resource, Women in Management, 1989. The report of the Women in Education Conference 1989.

Business Women, David Clutterbuck and Marion Devine, Macmillan, 1987.

The Competitive Woman, Janet Cameron, Mercury, 1988. A survival guide for the woman who aims to be boss.

Returning to Work; Education and Training for Women, Longman, 1987.

How to be a Successful Business Woman, Janet MacDonald, Methuen, 1987.

Projecting Your Image, Pat Roberts, Mercury, 1991. A practical guide to styling for success.

Women Working It Out. Jane Chapman, COIC, 1990. For women thinking of returning to work, education or training. Combines information and advice, plus case studies of women who have balanced all their commitments. Very readable.

Job Hunting for Women, Margaret Wallis, Kogan Page, 1987. A useful book combining information and advice for women of all ages, from first-time graduate jobhunters to women returning to work. Its aim is to boost confidence.

FOR CAREERS INFORMATION

Equal Opportunities: A Careers Guide for Women and Men, Ruth Miller and Anna Alston, Penguin (8th Edition), 1987. Well researched, comprehensive, well laid out, non-sexist. Particularly useful for women returning to paid work and the job changer.

Part-Time Work, Judith Humphries, Kogan Page, 1986. A guide to your rights, opportunities and conditions of work and all the practical aspect of working part-time.

Occupations, COIC. Published annually. A guide to occupations in the professions, industry, commerce and the public services.

Jobs and Careers After Advanced Levels, Mary Munro, Hobsons Press, 1987.

Job Sharing: A Practical Guide, Pam Walton, Kogan Page, 1990. A valuable book for those wishing to pursue an active career on a part-time basis, and for employers, on the concept of job sharing.

FOR EDUCATIONAL AND TRAINING INFORMATION

Directory of Further Education. The Comprehensive Guide to Courses in UK Polytechnics and Colleges. James Tomlinson and David Weigall (Eds.), CRAC, Hobsons Press Annually. This really is comprehensive – although it gives little detailed course information. It contains courses at all levels and in almost every academic or vocational area in maintained institutions outside universities. Particularly useful for non-advanced further education.

The Student Book: An Applicant's Guide to UK Colleges, Polytechnics and Universities. K. H. Boehm and J. L. Spalding (Eds.), Papermac. Annually. Contains information on places where you can study for a degree. Includes a description of each institution and the main subjects on offer.

Compendium of Advanced Courses in Colleges of Further and Higher Education, Ed. R. Eberhard, London and South-Eastern Regional Advisory Council For Further Education. Annually. Very comprehensive summary of all posts 'A' Level (and equivalent) courses in maintained institutions outside universities.

Which Degree? Newpoint Publishing Company. Published biannually in June. Five volumes covering a range of related disciplines, including one which describes institutions and their facilities. Offers comprehensive, reliable summaries of the content of degree courses. A series of "composite mini prospectuses" for all institutions offering degree level work, grouped according to discipline.

Degree Course Guides, CRAC, Hobsons Press. Updated biannually. Each booklet covers one discipline or closely related disciplines and is revised every second year. Useful framework for choice of degree courses in all British institutions with helpful, comparative information on differences in content and emphasis, teaching methods, entrance requirements, etc.

Graduate Studies, CRAC Hobsons Press Annual Directory of all postgraduate courses. Comprehensive – unlike some "commercial" directories.

British Qualifications (21st edition), Ed. Priestley, Kogan Page 1991. Comprehensive list of all academic education, technical and professional qualifications including index of abbreviations and designatory letters.

Vocational Degree Course Offers, Brian W. Heap, Careers Consultants PCAS Handbook, Published annually by the Polytechnics Admissions System. P.O. Box 67, Cheltenham, Glos GL50 1HY.

UCCA Handbook. Published annually Universities Central Council on Admissions, P.O. Box 28, Cheltenham, Glos. GL50 1HY.

How to Choose Your Degree Course, Brian W. Heap (Ed.), Career Consultants, 1987.

Graduate Opportunities: A Guide to Opportunities for Students at Universities and other Institutes of Higher Education, 1988. B. Leask (Ed.), Newpoint Publishing Company, 1987.

Second Chances: Guide to Adult Education and Training Opportunities, COIC, 1990. An annual guide to adult education and training opportunities. Excellent.

The Open Learning Directory, The Training Agency, 1989. Department of Employment. A guide to the range of open learning available today.

Part-Time Degrees, Diplomas & Certificates, Malcolm Tight CRAC. This book covers part-time higher education courses at Universities, Polytechnics and Colleges.

FOR TIME OUT

A Year Off.... A Year On?: A Guide to Jobs, Voluntary Service and Working Holidays During Your Education. Hobsons Press, 1987. Useful for students and anybody else who wants to spend up to a year in temporary or voluntary work.

The International Directory of Voluntary Work, David Woodworth, Vacation Work, 1989. Covers a wide range of full and part-time, home-based and voluntary opportunities in the UK and overseas.

Taking A Year Off, Val Butcher & Chris Swanson, Trotman & Co. Ltd., 1989. An excellent book which helps individuals recognise their particular needs and the best use of their time when taking a year off.

FOR JOB CHANGING

Changing Your Job After 35. Godfrey Golzen, Kogan Page, 1988. One of the better guides to this area. Comprehensive, though written mainly for executives in mid-career.

Working Abroad: The 'Daily Telegraph' Guide to Living and Working Overseas, Godfrey Golzen and Margaret Stewart, 1987.

The Directory of Jobs and Careers Abroad, Vacation Work, 1989.

Goodbye 9–5, Michael Syrett, New Opportunity Press, 1985.

Directory of Work & Study in Developing Countries. Vacation Work, 1990. A reference book which covers employment, voluntary work and study opportunities in the Third World.

Finding the Right Job, Anne Segall with William Greason, BBC, 1990. This book includes information on all aspects of the job search from writing the initial application form to making the right impression at interview.

FOR JOB SEARCHING

Reference books and directories are a valuable source of information in job searches. They are usually available in main branches of your Public Library Service, but if you have access to a University or Polytechnic Library you will also find many specialist reference books not readily available in the local library.

The source directory is:

Current British Directories (CBD)
Lists directories published in the British Isles: "directories which enable a searcher to locate, identify or obtain further information about a person, organisation or other unit; or which provide lists of persons and organisations in a particular industry, trade or group, or in a specific area."

Some of the main reference books are:

Kompass (3 volumes: especially Vol. 2 – Company Information)
UK Companies are listed alphabetically and by town within countries. The company information includes key executives, address, telephone number, number of employees and product details. (Further details of products are given in Vol. 1 with financial data in Vol. 1) Volume 1 also includes a list of Trade Associations (by products and services) with the address, telephone number and director or Secretary of those Trade Associations listed.

Key British Enterprises, Dun & Bradstreet Limited, commonly called 'Dun & Bradstreet' (3 volumes):

Volumes 1 & 2
Section 1: Businesses in alphabetical order. Reference volume
Section 2: Part 1 lists products and services in alphabetical order with the relevant Industrial Classification number. Part 2 lists the Industrial Classification codings with brief description of the trade covered.
Section 3: Gives the names of the businesses under each Industrial Classification.
Section 4: Enables the reader to identify those businesses in a particular classification in a chosen county.

Kelly's Business Directory
Classified list of manufacturers, merchants, wholesalers and firms offering services to commerce and industry. (Kelly's also have a number of specialised directories, e.g. Oil & Gas Industry).

Directory of British Associations
List trade associations, scientific and technical societies, research organisations, chambers of trade, agricultural societies, trade unions, cultural, sports and welfare organisations in the UK and Republic of Ireland. Gives name, address, telephone number and name of Hon. Secretary, Director or Director General.

Directory of Management Consultants in the UK
Full listing of firms offering business consultancy services giving specialisation, industry and geographical area.

British Consultants Bureau Directory
Gives details of all member firms, covering range of experience, expertise and disciplines.

Hambro Company Guide
Provides mainly financial information about 2,000 UK Companies plus names of directors, address, telephone number and, in many cases, number of employees.

Hambro Corporate Register
Contact details for 20,000 directors, top executives and advisers. Cross-referenced information on the people who manage and advise UK companies.

Moodys Handbook of Common Stock
Similar information to Hambro Guide but with more descriptive information about recent developments about United States quoted Companies.

Who Owns Whom (2 volumes and further 2 volumes for Continental Europe)
A directory showing links between Parent, Subsidiary and Associate Companies and Membership of Consortium.

Extel Handbook of Market Leaders
Covers all reports and information in respect of those companies which constitute the Financial Times Actuaries All Share Index.

Stock Exchange Official Year Book
Turnover, export sales and profits and balance sheets in terms of current cost accounting where published. Each entry includes details of principal subsidiary Companies.

The Times 1000
Annual review of the leading world industrial and financial companies.

Jordans Top 2000
Survey of Britain's privately owned companies.

Major Companies of – Europe
                    – The Arab World
Lists name, address and Company with name of directors, principal activities and financial information.

Standard and Poors Register
Register of US Corporations, Directors and Executives.

Personnel Manager's Yearbook. Lists recruitment and training organisations and management consultants. Gives name of the individual responsible for recruitment in 4,500 of the country's largest organisations.

Executive Grapevine
Lists Executive Search firms and recruitment consultants.

Examples of specialist directories
Bankers, Almanac and Year Book
BRAD, Advertiser and Agency List
Directory of Directors
Hollis. Press and Public Relations Annual
Insurance Directory and Year Book
The Retail Directory
the various professional institutions' directories
eg. Accountants, Lawyers, Architects, Quantity Surveyors.

WHERE TO CONSULT DIRECTORIES

City Business Library, 55 Basinghall Street, London EC2V 5BX. (071-638 8215/6); maintains a substantial stock of British Commonwealth and foreign directories.

The Statistics and Market Intelligence Library, 1 Victoria Street, London, SW1H OET. (071-215 5444); has the best available collection in London of Commonwealth, foreign and international directories.

The British Library (Science Reference Library), Holborn Branch, 25 Southampton Buildings, London WC2A 1AW. (071-405 8721); has good stocks of British and foreign directories in the fields of industry, science and technology.

Holborn Library (London Borough of Camden), 32–38 Theobald's Road, London WC1X 8PA. (071-405 2705)

Outside London, all large cities, particularly Birmingham, Bristol, Glasgow, Leeds, Liverpool, Manchester, Nottingham and Sheffield have extensive collections of directories.

FOR SELF-EMPLOYMENT
Working For Yourself: The 'Daily Telegraph' Guide to Self-Employment. Godfrey Golzen, Kogan Page, 1987. Sound advice, information and case studies.

Workers' Co-operative Handbook: A Comprehensive Guide to Setting Up a Workers' Co-operative. Peter Cockerton and Ann Whyatt, ICOM Co-Publications, 1986.

Home Earner: The Complete Guide to Money-making Ideas from Home. Christine Brady, Corgi, 1987. A source book on how to make money from working at home.

Taking Up a Franchise, Colin Barrow and Godfrey Golzen, Kogan Page, 1988.

Just for Starters: A handbook for small-scale business opportunities. A Bollard, Intermediate Technology Publications, 1985. (Also, illustrated paperback). Profiles of 33 industries where small enterprises could be profitable.

'Economist' Pocket Entrepreneur, Colin Barrow, Blackwell, 1987.

Earning Money at Home, E. Rudinger (Ed.), Consumers' Association, Hodder, 1986.

Starting Your Own Business, E Rudinger (Ed.), Consumers' Association, Hodder, 1986.

'Guardian' Guide to Running a Small Business. Clive Woodcock (Ed.), Kogan Page, 1987.

Starting a Business on a Shoestring, Michael Syrett and Chris Dunn, Penguin, 1988.

FOR UNEMPLOYED PEOPLE
Job Seeking for Unemployed Graduates. One of AGCAS Information Booklets freely available from most Higher Education careers services.

New Unemployment Handbook, Guy Dauncey, National Extension College, 1987.

NETWORKS AND SOURCES OF HELP AND ADVICE FOR LEARNING
Community Education Courses.
Open University Courses exist on Work Choices (based on Build Your Own Rainbow), Planned Retirement, Parents and Teenagers, Health Choices, Consumer Decisions, etc. Each course is designed primarily for a specific target group and consists of a short home-study course with text book, audio cassettes, information, accompanying notes and a set of computer marked assignments. Write for details to ASCO, PO Box 76, The Open University, Milton Keynes, MK7 6AA.

Open University.
For details of all their programmes write to the Open University, Walton Hall, Milton Keynes, MK7 6AA.

L.E.A. Courses
Every L.E.A. has part-time adult education classes. For a prospectus try your local library, the L.E.A. Offices or the Workers' Educational Association in your area.

University Extra-Mural Classes.
A number of Universities have extra-mural or adult education departments offering courses to the public. Newer ones have continuing education departments. Some Polytechnics and Colleges of Higher Education also have similar facilities.

TV and Radio.
Both the BBC and ITV produce a variety of education programmes, some of them with back-up material. Channel 4 has a special

objective of encouraging viewers to learn at home. For information write to:

Educational Liaison Officer, Channel 4 Television, 60 Charlotte Street, London W1P 2AX.
Education Officer (Information), IBA, 70 Brompton Road, London SW3 1EY. (071-584 7011)
Insight Information, BBC, Broadcasting House, London W1A 1AA

For information about educational programmes on the radio write to:

Radio Publicity, BBC, Broadcasting House, London W1A 1AA or telephone 071-580 4468 ext 2620.

The Open College.
The Open College is an independent educational charity dedicated to providing flexible training courses to help individuals enhance their vocational skills and improve performance in the workplace. Open College courses cover management and supervisory training, technical and engineering, health care and accountancy, as well as essential vocational skills. Contact the Open College, Freepost TK1006, Brentford, Middlesex TW8 8BR (0800 300760).

FOR CAREER AND EDUCATION ADVICE AND INFORMATION

Careers Service. Every local education authority has one. They are very overstretched in carrying out their statutory responsibilities for young people, but many of them do manage to provide a guidance service for adults. Look in the telephone directory under Careers Service. The service is free.

National Advisory Centre on Careers for Women, 8th Floor, Artillery House, Artillery Row, London SW1P 1RT.

Job Centres. This is the first place to ask about all government training opportunities.

TAP (Training Access Point), TAP Employment Department, Information & Advice Services Unit, St. Mary's House, c/o Moorfoot, Sheffield S1 4PO. (0742 597344) TAP was set up for the awareness and take-up of work-related education and training opportunities. It offers: detailed information on a wide range of learning opportunities; quick access to information through conveniently located and easy to use terminals; support in putting together a learning programme which meets individual or company needs. The new Training & Enterprise Councils (TECs) will be involved in the contribution TAP can make in meeting the needs of individuals and businesses in their locality.

ECCTIS (Education Counselling and Credit Transfer Information Services), Fulton House, Jessop Avenue, Cheltenham, Glos. GL50 3SH. (0242 518724) A computerised database offering a service to students, prospective students and students' advisors, to provide information to help match individual needs to available courses leading to recognised qualifications. This includes information about courses available in a particular area of study together with normal minimum qualifications for entry and, where appropriate, alternative or partial qualifications which have been found to be acceptable.

MARIS ON LINE (Materials and Resources Information Service) Bank House, 1 St. Mary's Street, Ely, Cambridge, CB7 4ER (0353 661284). MARIS is an on line service that can produce print-outs describing open learning materials (books, tapes, videos, software, etc.) for individuals who request it.

PICKUP Training Directory, Guildford Education Services, 32 Castle Street, Guildford GU1 3UW (0483 579454). A database of 25,000 entries. It provides information on both public and private sector vocational short courses and other training opportunities. Available on Prestel and MARIS on line micro computer floppy disk, compact disk and annually in print with Macmillan.

NATIONAL ASSOCIATION OF EDUCATIONAL GUIDANCE FOR ADULTS

National Educational Guidance Initiative. Sponsored by the DES and the Training Agency. The initiative remit encompasses five major areas of work. Consultancy to Local Bodies; Liaison with National Bodies; Training & Development; Dissemination & Strategic Development. Latest publication *Educational Guidance*

for Adults 1988–89 (UDACE 1990) presents a national overview of educational guidance activity. With the CNAA NEGI is exploring the development of guidance in H. E. institutions. NEGI/UDACE, YHAFHE, Bowling Green Terrace, Leeds LS11 9SX.

The National Association for Education Guidance for Adults (NAEGA) promotes the delivery of high quality educational guidance for adults. There are over 80 services nationwide offering independent and impartial information, advice and counselling to adults wishing to return to education and training. For a copy of the Directory of Services (price £2), contact Anne Docherty, Secretary, The Mews Cottage, 7 Botanic Crescent Lane, Glasgow, G20 8AA.

FOR VOLUNTARY WORK

British Executive Service Overseas, 10 Belgrave Square, London SW1.

Voluntary Service Overseas, 317 Putney Bridge Road, London SW15 2PN. (081 780 2266)

Oxfam Voluntary Service Council, 274 Banbury Road, Oxford OX2 7DZ.

National Council for Voluntary Organisations, 26 Bedford Square, London WC1B 3HU. (071 636 4066)

Central Register of Charities, Charity Commissioners, 57–60 Haymarket, London SW1 OPZ. (071 210 3000).

GAP Activity Projects Ltd., 7 Kings Road, Reading, Berkshire RG1 3AA.

Community Service Volunteers, 237 Pentonville Road, London N19NJ. (071-278 6601)

International Voluntary Service, 162 Upper New Walk, Leicester LE1 7QA. (0533 549430)

London Voluntary Service Council, 68 Chalton Street, London NW1 IJR. (071-388 0241)

FOR ALTERNATIVE WORK PATTERNS

New Ways to Work, 309 Upper Street, London N1 OPD. (ring 071-226 4026 between 10 a.m. and 1 p.m. Tues., Wed. and Fri.). This produces leaflets on job-sharing and can put you in touch with job-sharing groups around the country.

Industrial Common Ownership Movement, Vassalli House, 20 Central Road, Leeds LS1 6DE. (0532 461737) Advice and information on how to set up and run worker co-operatives.

Centre for Employment Initiatives Ltd, Unit 13, 44 Pearlham St. London WC2H 9LA. (071-240 8901)

Part-Time Careers Ltd, 10 Golden Square, London W1R 2AF. (071-437 3103/734 0559)

FOR SELF-EMPLOYMENT

Small Firms Centres (Freephone 2444) will put you in touch with local initiatives to help people thinking of setting up their own businesses. They also provide an initial free consultation service.

Business in the Community, 227a City Road, London EC1V 1LX. (071-253 3716) They will tell you if there are any Enterprise Agencies in your part of the country.

Small Business Bureau, 32 Smith Square, London WC1P 3HH.

Rural Development Commission, 141 Castle Street, Salisbury, Wiltshire SP1 3TP. (0722 336255) Offers help to people thinking of starting up businesses or currently operating in an English rural area.

Enterprise Allowance Scheme. A scheme to help unemployed people start up their own business. If you are unemployed, you can be paid £40 a week for up to a year while you are starting up. Ask for details at your local Job Centre.

Confederation of British Industry (CBI), Centrepoint, 103 New Oxford Street, London WC1A 1DU (071-379 7400) Includes Small Firms Council.

Crafts Council, 1 Oxendon Street, London SW1X 4AT.(071-930 4811)

London Enterprise Agency, Small Business Counselling and Training, 4 Snow Hill, London EC1A 2BS. (071-236 3000)

National Chamber of Trade, Enterprise House, Pack and Prime Lane, Henley-on-Thames, Oxon RG9 1TU. (0491 576161) Headquarters of Chambers of Trade to be found throughout Britain.

Development Board for Rural Wales, Ladywell House, Newtown, Powys, SY16 1JB. (0686 626965) Promotes the economic and social development of mid-Wales; gives advice to those wanting to set up in business.

Small Business Unit, Welsh Development Agency, Treforest Industrial Estate, Pontypridd, Mid-Glamorgan CF3 75UT. (0443 841131)

National Federation of Self-Employed and Small Businesses Ltd, (Head Office) 32 St Anne's Road West, Lytham St Anne's, Lancs. FY8 1NY. (0253 720911) (Press and Parliamentary Office) 140 Lower Marsh, London SE1 7AE. (071-928 9272)

New Enterprise Network, 3 Stonehill, Chobham, Surrey GU24 8HP.

Scottish Retail Federation, 203 Pitt Street, Glasgow GL2 7JG.

Northern Ireland Development Board, Local Enterprise Development Unit, Lamont House, Purdys Lane, Belfast BT8. 17 The Diamond, Londonderry, BP48 6BR

Scottish Development Agency, Rosebury House, Haymarket Terrace, Edinburgh EH12 5EX. (031 337 9595)

Highlands and Islands Development Board, 20 Bridge Street, Inverness IV1 1QR. (0463 234171)

URBED, Enterprise Development, Tress House, 3 Stamford Street, London SE1 9NT. (071-401 2099)

FOR UNEMPLOYED PEOPLE

National Development Union, c/o Birmingham Settlement, 318 Summer Lane, Birmingham B19 3RL. (021 359 2113) A network of unemployment groups designed to give practical help, support and training to those who want to set up self-help groups.

Unemployed Workers Centres, TUC Unemployed Workers' Centres, Congress House, Great Russell Street, London WC1B 3LS. (071-636 4030) These are to be found around the UK and they offer advice for those unemployed and those facing redundancy.

FOR RETIREMENT

Pre-Retirement Association, 19 Undine Street, London SW17 899. (081-767 3225)

REACH (Retired Executives Action Clearing House) 89 Southwark Street, London SE1 OHD. (071-928 0452)

Action Resource Centre, Cap House 9–12 Long Lane, London EC1A 9HD. (071-726 8987)

Business in the Community, 227a City Road, London EC1V 1LX. (071-253 3716)

Success After Sixty, 40 Old Bond Street, London W1X 3AF. (071-629 0672)

BESO (British Executive Service Overseas), Mount Barrow Hall, 16–20 Elizabeth Street, London SW1W 9RB. (071-730 0022)

FOR PEOPLE WITH DISABILITIES

RADAR (Royal Association for Disability and Rehabilitation), 25 Mortimer Street London WIN 8AB. (071-637 5400) Provides a job search information pack.

Opportunities for the Disabled, Head Office, 1 Bank Building, Prince's Street, London EC2R 8EU. (071-726 4963) They provide counselling and training advice on education and employment, as well as trying to find jobs for disabled people.

Disablement Income Group, Mill Mead Business Centre, Mill Mead Road, London N17 9QU. (081-801 8013) Advice for disabled people.

The Disabled Living Foundation, 380 Harrow Road, London W9 2HU. (071-289 6111)

Disability Alliance (see local telephone directory). Produce an excellent handbook.

FOR BEREAVEMENT AND LONELINESS

CRUSE (support and advice for the bereaved), Cruse House, Sheen Road, Richmond, Surrey.

Old Friends (introduction agency for the over 40s), 18a Highbury New Park, London N5 2DB.

Samaritans (see telephone directory): 17 Uxbridge Road, Slough SL1 1AN

FOR MOVING HOUSE

National Federation of Housing Associations, 30–32 Southampton Street, London WC2F 7HF.

FOR WOMEN

Women in Business, 43a Lower Addiscombe Road, Croydon CRO 6PQ. (081-688 3332) Organises large exhibitions including much information on careers.

Women in Management, 64 Marryat Road, Wimbledon, London SW19 5BN. (081-9456 1238)

Women in Enterprise, 26 Bond Street, Wakefield, W. Yorkshire.

PEOPLE OF MINORITY ETHNIC GROUPS

Fullemploy Training Ltd, Central Office, 102 Park Village East, London NW1 3SP. (071-387 1222) Part of Fullemploy Group Ltd, which also includes Fullemploy Consultancy, Fullemploy Enterprise and Fullemploy Publications. Aims to provide vocational educational and training, principally to adults of minority ethnic origin, in order that they may compete more effectively in the wider economic community.

FOR RELATIONSHIPS

Relate, 7A Sheep Street, Rugby. Formerly the National Marriage Guidance Council.

FOR CARERS OF ELDERLY RELATIVES

Age Concern, Bernard Sunley House, Pitcairn Road, Mitcham, Surrey.

National Association of Carers, 58 New Road, Chatham, Kent, ME4 4QR.

National Council for the Single Woman and her Dependants, 29 Chilworth Mews, London W2 3RG

National Council for Carers and their Elderly Dependants, 29 Chilworth Mews, London W2 3RG.

consists of the 24 JOB FAMILIES referred to in the section WHO AM I?
You can match your skills and interest against the jobs mentioned here.

Watch Point

JOB FAMILIES WATCHPOINTS

- Don't forget that it is possible to enter some of the jobs in all of the job families by a number of different routes.

- For some jobs experience can compensate for a lack of formal qualifications.

- It is not always possible to enter jobs even if you do have all the necessary qualifications.

- Jobs with the same title can be found at a number of different levels.

- In all job families it is possible to move between levels as well as between jobs.

- Even though a job family may be found in a particular region of the World of Employment Map, there could be other skills and interests required for individual occupations within this family. Therefore, some of the occupations listed will be followed by a letter in brackets. This suggests that this occupation would also have something in common with the jobs listed under the job family in brackets and its region.
  It is always difficult to fit jobs into neat and tidy categories which is why we have done this cross-referencing. The purpose of this approach is to suggest some alternatives that you may not have previously considered and that could have relevance to your skills and interests.

Map Region		OCCUPATIONAL GROUP AND JOB FAMILY NAMES	Page No. for Job Family
		Business Sales and Management	
1	A	Marketing and Selling	p 154
2	B	Management and Planning	p 154
1	C	Retail Sales and Services	p 155
		Business Operations	
4	D	Administration & Information Management	p 156
3	E	Cash Handling, Finance and Accounting	p 156
5	F	Office Machine Operation	p 157
5	G	Storage, Dispatching and Delivery	p 157
		Technologies and Trades	
6	H	General Services	p 158
6	I	Repairing and Servicing Home and Office Equipment	p 159
6	J	Growing and Caring for Plants/Animals	p 159
6	K	Construction and Maintenance	p 160
6	L	Transport Equipment Operation	p 160
7	M	Engineering Processing and Other Applied Technologies	p 161

Map Region		OCCUPATIONAL GROUP AND JOB FAMILY NAMES	Page No. for Job Family
		Natural, Social and Medical Sciences	
8	N	Natural Sciences and Mathematics	p 162
12	O	Medicine and Medical Technologies	p 163
9	P	Social Sciences and Legal Services	p 163
		Arts and Media	
10	Q	Performing Arts	p 164
11	R	Literary	p 164
10	S	Art and Design	p 165
12	T	Popular Entertainment and Professional Sport	p 165
		Social, Health and Personal Services	
12	U	Education and Social Services	p 166
12	V	Nursing and Personal Care	p 166
3	W	Catering and Personal Services	p 167
4	X	Security and Protective Services	p 167

For detailed information on any of the jobs look at the Resources Section on page 148 – Career Information. This will suggest bodies and places where you can get this.

CHART 1 BUSINESS SALES AND MANAGEMENT

JOB FAMILY	LEVEL 1	LEVEL 2:	LEVEL 3:	LEVEL 4:
	Unskilled and semiskilled jobs. These usually need no specific educational qualifications. Practical abilities are more important.	Skilled practical and clerical jobs. These usually involve greater on-the-job training and may require some passes at GCSE/S grade.	Supervisory and middle management, technician and some professional occupations come into this category. Occupations in this group usually require at least GCSE/S grade (A–C/1–3) and often A levels/H grade passes. Completion of some further training – often full-time – is usually necessary.	Professional and higher management occupations. Entry to these occupations usually requires the successful completion of a recognised degree or diploma course or extensive experience and highly developed skills at an equivalent level. Postgraduate training is often desirable.
A Marketing and Selling	Fashion/Photographer's Model (Q) Telephone Sales Person	Sales Representative Car Salesperson Auctioneer Insurance Agent Travel Agency Clerk (D) Sales Negotiator (Estate Agency) Publicity Officer Classified Advertising Sales Agent Market Research Interviewer Tourist Information Officer (W) Fashion/Photographer's Model (Q) Airline Passenger Service Assistant (D)	Advertisement Manager Account Executive (Advertising Agency) Insurance Broker Stockbroker's Clerk (E) Marketing Executive Public Relations Officer Recruiting Officer (MOD) Literary Agent (R) Media Executive Estate Agent Advertising Copywriter (R) Public Relations Officer (R) Ship & Air Broker (G&E)	Marketing Manager (B) Senior Editor (Publishing) (R) Market Research Analyst Estate Agent Commodity Broker Company Sales Manager Stockbroker (E) Public Relations Officer (R) Tourist Information Officer (W) Market Maker (Stock Exchange) (E) Ship & Air Broker (G & E)
B Management and Planning	No jobs available at this level	Appeals Officer (Charity) Party Agent (Political) Sheltered Workshop Supervisor Betting Shop Manager Work Study Assistant (D)	Box Officer Manager Housing Manager Laundry and Dry Cleaning Manager Organisation and Methods Officer Work Study Officer Contract Manager Training Officer (U) Purchasing Officer Constituency Agent Cinema Manager Betting Shop Manager Car Sales Manager (C) Land Agent Bingo Club Manager Personnel Officer (U) Traffic Manager (L) Market Garden Manager (J) Retail Manager (C)	Health Service Manager (D) Personnel Manager (U) Museum/Art Gallery Curator (S) Local Government Administrator (D) Company Secretary (E) Contract Manager Training Manager (U) Purchasing Officer Constituency Agent Betting Shop Manager Housing Manager Town Planner (S) Higher Executive Officer/Executive Officer (Civil Service) (D) Diplomatic Service – Executive Officer Company Registrar Prison Governor (X)

Remember the
Watch Point

The distinction by occupational level is adapted from the classification used in 'Job Ideas', Careers and Occupational Information Centre, 1982; also with reference to Standard Occupational Classification HMSO 1990.

JOB FAMILY	LEVEL 1	LEVEL 2	LEVEL 3:	LEVEL 4:
	Unskilled and semiskilled jobs. These usually need no specific educational qualifications. Practical abilities are more important.	Skilled practical and clerical jobs. These usually involve greater on-the-job training and may require some passes at GCSE/S grade.	Supervisory and middle management, technician and some professional occupations come into this category. Occupations in this group usually require at least GCSE/S grade (A–C/1–3) and often A levels/H grade passes. Completion of some further training – often full-time – is usually necessary.	Professional and higher management occupations. Entry to these occupations usually requires the successful completion of a recognised degree or diploma course or extensive experience and highly developed skills at an equivalent level. Postgraduate training is often desirable.
			Farm Manager (J)	Chief Fire Officer (X)
			Funeral Director (U)	Chief Constable (X)
			Assistant Director (Theatre/TV) (Q)	Chief Security Officer (Private Undertaking) (X)
			Theatre Manager (Q)	Transport Manager (G)
			Producer (Radio/TV) (Q)	Planning and Development Surveyor (K)
			Touring Manager (Entertainment) (T)	Market Garden Manager (J)
			Team Manager (Sports & Games) (T)	Farm Manager (J)
			Trainer (Private Sector) (U)	Horticultural Manager (J)
			Casting Director (Q)	Fish Farmer/Manager (J)
				Principal Nursing Officer (V)
				Community Medical Officer (O)
				Chief Executive (Local Authority) (P)
				Zoo Manager (J)
				Stable Manager (J)
				Production Manager (M)
				Quarry Manager (M)
				Director (Theatre/TV) (Q)
				Producers (TV/Radio) (Q)
				Trainer (Private Sector) (U)
				Marketing Manager (A)
				Funeral Director (U)
C Retail Sales and Services	Retail Assistant	Bookseller	Retail Manager (B)	Buyer (Retail Distribution)
	Shelf Filler (Supermarket)	Antique Dealer (S)	Car Sales Manager (B)	Retail Pharmacist (O)
	Forecourt Attendant (I-)	Musical Instrument Sales	Antique Dealer (S)	Retail Manager
	Car Rental Salesman/woman	Sales Supervisor	Publican/Bar Manager (W)	Antique Dealer (S)
	Milk Roundsman/woman	Roundsman Supervisor	Fast Food Manager (W)	
	Cash Till Operator	Store Demonstrator		
	Trainee Butcher (W)	Butcher (W)		
	Floristry Assistant (S)	Florist (S)		
	Waiter/Waitress (W)	Window Dresser/Display Assistant (S)		
	Barman/Woman (W)	Publican/Bar Manager (W)		
	Counter Service Assistant (W)	Beauty Consultant (W)		
		Hairdresser (S & W)		
		Air Steward/Stewardess (W)		

Remember the WATCH Point

155

The distinction by occupational level is adapted from the classification used in 'Job Ideas' Careers and Occupational Information Centre, 1982; also with reference to Standard Occupational Classification HMSO 1990.

JOB FAMILY	LEVEL 1	LEVEL 2	LEVEL 3	LEVEL 4:
	Unskilled and semiskilled jobs. These usually need no specific educational qualifications. Practical abilities are more important.	Skilled practical and clerical jobs. These usually involve greater on-the-job training and may require some passes at GCSE/S grade.	Supervisory and middle management, technician and some professional occupations come into this category. Occupations in this group usually require at least GCSE/S grade (A–C/1–3) and often A levels/H grade passes. Completion of some further training – often full-time – is usually necessary.	Professional and higher management occupations. Entry to these occupations usually requires the successful completion of a recognised degree or diploma course or extensive experience and highly developed skills at an equivalent level. Postgraduate training is often desirable.
D Administration and Information Management	General Clerk Messenger (G) Filing Clerk	Correspondence Clerk Control Clerk (Data Processing) Library Clerk (Automatic Data Records) Press Cuttings Clerk Bilingual Secretary (R) Receptionist Library Assistant (R) Secretary Legal Secretary (P) Medical Secretary (V) Farm Secretary (J) Administrative Officer/Assistant (Civil Service) Clerk/Typist Typist/Word Processor Operator Clerical Worker (Local Government) Customer Service Clerk Travel Agency Clerk (A) Airline Passenger Service Assistant (A) Ward Clerk (V) Medical Records Clerk (V) Postal Officer Wages Clerk (E) School Secretary (U) Court Officer (P) Justices' Clerks Assistant (P) Accounts Clerk (E) Hotel Receptionist (W) Bank Clerk (E) Audit Clerk (E) Book-Keeper Cost Clerk (E) Sales & Statistics Clerk (E) Invoice Clerk (E) Building Society Clerk (E) Sales Ledger Clerk (E) Tax Officer (E) Postal Officer (E) Air Traffic Control Assistant (L) Insurance Clerk (E) Work Study Assistant (B)	Supervisor (General & Clerical Occupations) (E) Executive Secretary Executive Officer/Administrative Trainee (Civil Service) Local Government Administrator (B) Secretary/Personal Assistant Computer Programmer (N) Supervisor (Cash Handling & Financial Occupations) (E) Organising Secretary (Voluntary Organisation) (U) Housing Officer (U) Supervisor (Computer Operations) (F)	Librarian (R) Archivist Information Officer/Scientist (N) Executive Secretary Computer Programmer (N) Systems Analyst (N) Higher Executive Officer/Executive Officer (Civil Service) (B) Health Service Manager (B) Local Government Administrator (B) Postal Executive/Executive Officer (E) Air Traffic Control Officer (L) Environmental Health Officer (U&H) Trading Standards Officer (U&H) Banker – Corporate, Domestic, Merchant & International (E) Bank Manager (E) Chartered Accountant (E) Management Accountant (E) Public Finance Accountant (E) Certified Accountant (E) Building Society Manager (E) Patent Agent (H) Economist (N) Health & Safety Inspector (U&H)

Remember the Watch Point

The distinction by occupational level is adapted from the classification used in 'Job Ideas', Careers and Occupational Information Centre, 1982; also with reference to Standard Occupational Classification

	LEVEL 1	LEVEL 2	LEVEL 3	LEVEL 4
	Unskilled and semiskilled jobs. These usually need no specific educational qualifications. Practical abilities are more important.	Skilled practical and clerical jobs. These usually involve greater on-the-job training and may require some passes at GCSE/S grade.	Supervisory and middle management, technician and some professional occupations come into this category. Occupations in this group usually require at least GCSE/S grade (A–C/1–3) and often A levels/H grade passes. Completion of some further training – often full-time – is usually necessary.	Professional and higher management occupations. Entry to these occupations usually requires the successful completion of a recognised degree or diploma course or extensive experience and highly developed skills at an equivalent level. Postgraduate training is often desirable.

CHART 2 BUSINESS OPERATIONS

	LEVEL 1	LEVEL 2	LEVEL 3	LEVEL 4
E Cash Handling, Finance and Accounting	Cashier/Rent Collector Coin Collector (Meters) Fee Collector Credit Club Agent	Accounts Clerk (D) Wages Clerk (D) Bank Clerk (D) Audit Clerk (D) Book Keeper (D) Cost Clerk (D) Sales Statistics Clerk (D) Invoice Clerk (D) Building Society Clerk (D) Settler, Bookmaking Tax Officer (D) Accounting Technician Sales Ledger Clerk (D) Postal Officer (D) Insurance Salesman/woman Insurance Clerk (D)	Supervisor (General & Clerical Occupations) (D) Supervisor (Cash Handling & Financia Occupations) (D) Foreign Exchange Clerk (Banking) Securities Clerk Stockbroker's Clerk (A) Pensions Information Officer Rent Officer Accounting Technician Wages Manager Financial Accountant Claims Official (Insurance) Insurance Surveyor Loss Adjuster (Insurance) Ship & Air Broker (A&G)	Banker – Corporate, Domestic, Merchant & International (D) Bank Manager (D) Actuary Licensed Broker (Securities) Investment Analyst (Stock Exchange) Company Registrar Registrar of Stocks and Bonds Tax Consultant Tax Inspector Chartered Accountant (D) Management Accountant (D) Public Finance Accountant (D) Certified Accountant (D) Stockbroker (A) Postal Executive/Executive Officer (D) Building Society Manager (D) Insurance Underwriter Insurance Broker Market Maker (Stock Exchange) (A) Pensions Broker Pensions Consultant Auditor Company Secretary (B) Ship & Air Broker (G&A)

Remember the
Watch Point

157

The distinction by occupational level is adapted from the classification used in 'Job Ideas', Careers and Occupational Information Centre, 1982; also with reference to Standard Occupational Classification HMSO 1990.

JOB FAMILY	LEVEL 1	LEVEL 2	LEVEL 3:	LEVEL 4:
	Unskilled and semiskilled jobs. These usually need no specific educational qualifications. Practical abilities are more important.	Skilled practical and clerical jobs. These usually involve greater on-the-job training and may require some passes at GCSE/S grade.	Supervisory and middle management, technician and some professional occupations come into this category. Occupations in this group usually require at least GCSE/S grade (A–C/1–3) and often A levels/H grade passes. Completion of some further training – often full-time – is usually necessary.	Professional and higher management occupations. Entry to these occupations usually requires the successful completion of a recognised degree or diploma course or extensive experience and highly developed skills at an equivalent level. Postgraduate training is often desirable.
F Office Machine Operation	Calculating Machine Operator Reprographic Technician Office Machinery Operator	PABX Operator Data Processing Operator Reprographic Technician Switchboard Operator Typist/Word Processor Operator Computer Operator Telex Operator Telephonist	Supervisor (Computer Operations) D	
G Storage, Dispatching and Delivery	Mail Sorter Postman/Woman Messenger (D) Store Keeper Warehouse Worker Motor Cycle Messenger Van Driver Furniture Remover	Import Clerk Stock Controller Chartering Clerk (Air Bookings) Load Planner Export Clerk Freight Forwarder Postroom Clerk Shipping Clerk Heavy Goods Vehicle Driver	Ship and Air Broker (E&A) Transport Manager (B) Wholesale Distribution Manager Cash & Carry Wholesale Manager	Transport Manager (B) Ship & Air Broker (E&A)

Remember the Watch Point

158

The distinction by occupational level is adapted from the classification used in 'Job Ideas', Careers and Occupational Information Centre, 1982; also with reference to Standard Occupational Classification HMSO 1990.

JOB FAMILY	LEVEL 1	LEVEL 2	LEVEL 3	LEVEL 4
	Unskilled and semiskilled jobs. These usually need no specific educational qualifications. Practical abilities are more important.	Skilled practical and clerical jobs. These usually involve greater on-the-job training and may require some passes at GCSE/S grade.	Supervisory and middle management, technician and some professional occupations come into this category. Occupations in this group usually require at least GCSE/S grade (A–C/1–3) and often A levels/H grade passes. Completion of some further training – often full-time – is usually necessary.	Professional and higher management occupations. Entry to these occupations usually requires the successful completion of a recognised degree or diploma course or extensive experience and highly developed skills at an equivalent level. Postgraduate training is often desirable.

CHART 3   TECHNOLOGIES & TRADES

JOB FAMILY	LEVEL 1	LEVEL 2	LEVEL 3	LEVEL 4

H General Services	Refuse Collector
	Removal Worker
	Window Cleaner
	Television Aerial Erector
	Bus Conductor
	Car Park Attendant
	Meter Reader
	Road Sweeper
	Ticket Collector
	Lavatory Attendant
	Funeral Director's Assistant
	Mortuary Attendant
	Laundry Worker
	Dry Cleaning Assistant
	Pest Control Officer
	Bill Poster
	Porter/Hotel Porter (W)
	Caretaker (W)
	Domestic Cleaner (W)
	Chimney Sweep (W)
	Window Cleaner (W)
	Sleeping Car Attendant (W)
	Lift Attendant (W)
		Appliance Demonstrator
		Patrolman/Woman (AA/RAC)
		Picture Framer
		Wig Maker (S)
		Document Repairer
		Driving Examiner
		Tricologist
		Undertaker/Embalmer
		Assistant Superintendent
		  (Cemetry/Crematorium)
		Taxidermist
		Carpet Fitter
		Lino Fitter
		Dressmaker (S)
		Tailor-Bespoke (S)
		Technical Assistant
		  (Environmental Health Office)
		Saddler
		Piano Tuner
		Pawnbroker
		Forecourt Attendant (C)
			Meat Inspector
			Kitchen Planner (S)
				Patent Agent (D)
				Health and Safety
				  Inspector (U&D)
				Environmental Health
				  Officer (U&D)
				Trading Standards Officer (U&D)

The distinction by occupational level is adapted from the classification used in 'Job Ideas', Careers and Occupational Information Centre, 1982; also with reference to Standard Occupational Classification HMSO 1990.

Remember the Watch Point

JOB FAMILY	LEVEL 1	LEVEL 2	LEVEL 3	LEVEL 4
	Unskilled and semiskilled jobs. These usually need no specific educational qualifications. Practical abilities are more important.	Skilled practical and clerical jobs. These usually involve greater on-the-job training and may require some passes at GCSE/S grade.	Supervisory and middle management, technician and some professional occupations come into this category. Occupations in this group usually require at least GCSE/S grade (A–C/1–3) and often A levels/H grade passes. Completion of some further training – often full-time – is usually necessary.	Professional and higher management occupations. Entry to these occupations usually requires the successful completion of a recognised degree or diploma course or extensive experience and highly developed skills at an equivalent level. Postgraduate training is often desirable.
I Repairing and Servicing Home and Office Equipment	Domestic Appliance Service Engineer: Camera Repairer Typewriter Mechanic	Piano Repairer Refrigeration and Air Conditioning Service Mechanic Watch and Clock Repairer Fire/Burglar Alarm Engineer Sewing Machine Engineer Antique Furniture Repairer (S) Musical Instrument Repairer Upholsterer (S) Installation and Maintenance Engineers for: Computers, Typewriters, Photocopiers, Dictaphones, Calculators, Franking Machines, Cash Registers, Postage Machines Domestic Appliance Service Engineers TV/Video and Radio Engineers Computer Service Engineer Telephone Technician Telecommunications Technician	Telephone Technician Telephone Engineer	Telephone Engineer
J Growing and Caring for Plants/Animals	Horticultural Worker Kennel Hand Stable Hand (T) Agricultural Worker Glasshouse Worker Orchard Worker Turf Layer Agricultural Machinery Operator Forest Worker Tree Feller Hedger Crop Harvester Groom Groundsman/Woman Dog Beautician	Veterinary Nurse Animal Technician Farrier Zoo Keeper Pigman/woman Poultryhand Gamekeeper Beekeeper Gardener Stockman/woman Agricultural Mechanic (M) Tree Surgeon Foreman/woman (Mixed Farming Workers) Nurseryman/woman Guide Dog Trainer Dog Beautician	Foreman/woman (Mixed Farming Workers) Arboriculturist Farm Manager (B) RSPCA/SPCA Inspector Fish Farmer Countryside Rangers and Wardens Forester Mobility Instructor (Guide Dogs for the Blind) (U) Water Bailiff Riding Instructor Market Garden Manager (B)	Botanist (N) Veterinary Surgeon (N) Zoologist (N) Farm Manager (B) Forest Officer/Forestry Manager Horticultural Manager (B) Scientific Officer (N) Landscape Architect (S) Market Garden Manager (B) Ecologist (N) Biologist (N) Zoo Manager (B) Fish Farmer/Manager (B) Ornithologist (N) Marine Biologist (N) Stable Manager (B) Soil Scientist (N)

Remember the Watch Point

160

The distinction by occupational level is adapted from the classification used in 'Job Ideas', Careers and Occupational Information Centre, 1982; also with reference to Standard Occupational Classification HMSO 1990.

JOB FAMILY	LEVEL 1	LEVEL 2	LEVEL 3	LEVEL 4:
	Unskilled and semiskilled jobs. These usually need no specific educational qualifications. Practical abilities are more important.	Skilled practical and clerical jobs. These usually involve greater on-the-job training and may require some passes at GCSE/S grade.	Supervisory and middle management, technician and some professional occupations come into this category. Occupations in this group usually require at least GCSE/S grade (A–C/1–3) and often A levels/H grade passes. Completion of some further training – often full-time – is usually necessary.	Professional and higher management occupations. Entry to these occupations usually requires the successful completion of a recognised degree or diploma course or extensive experience and highly developed skills at an equivalent level. Postgraduate training is often desirable.
		Fish Farm Technic an Water Keeper Groundsman/woman Farm Secretary (D) Jockey/Equestrian Rider (T) Golf Green Keeper (T) Riding Instructor (U&T) Arboriculturist Dog Handler (X)		
K Construction and Maintenance	Cleaning Contract Worker Builders Labourer Demolition Worker Fireplace Builder Floor and Wall Tiler Roofing Felt Fixer Fence Erector Mastic Asphalt Spreader Composition Floor Layer Sewer Worker Tile Layer Caretaker Construction – Labourer/Gang Worker	Electrician Stonemason Painter and Decorator Plumber Plasterer Boat Builder Cabinet Maker Construction Plant Fitter/ Contractors Plant Fepair & Maintenance Fitter Heating and Ventilatir g Fitter Scaffolder Roofer Slater/Tiler Streetmason/Pavier Monumental Mason Steeplejack Auto-Electrician Technical Assistant (Housing–Lccal Govt) Gas Fitter Wrought-Iron Smith (S) Bricklayer Carpenter & Joiner Glazier Thatcher Shop Fitter Stage Carpenter (Q)	Planning Technician Site Mar ager (Construction) Boat Builder Building Technician Civil Engineering Technician Architectural Technician (S) Surveying Technician	Structural Engineer (N) Civil Engineer (N) Architect (S) Surveyor – Quantity/Land/ Hydrographic Surveyor (N) Surveyor – Building (N) Planning/Development Surveyor (B)

Remember the Watch Point

The distinction by occupational level is adapted from the classification used in 'Job Ideas', Careers and Occupational Information Centre, 1982; also with reference to Standard Occupational Classification HMSO 1990.

JOB FAMILY	LEVEL 1	LEVEL 2	LEVEL 3	LEVEL 4:
	Unskilled and semiskilled jobs. These usually need no specific educational qualifications. Practical abilities are more important.	Skilled practical and clerical jobs. These usually involve greater on-the-job training and may require some passes at GCSE/S grade.	Supervisory and middle management, technician and some professional occupations come into this category. Occupations in this group usually require at least GCSE/S grade (A–C/1–3) and often A levels/H grade passes. Completion of some further training – often full-time – is usually necessary.	Professional and higher management occupations. Entry to these occupations usually requires the successful completion of a recognised degree or diploma course or extensive experience and highly developed skills at an equivalent level. Postgraduate training is often desirable.
L Transport Equipment Operation	Deck and Harbour Worker Lock Gate Keeper Guard (British Rail) Seaman/woman Drivers' Mate Deckhand Chauffeur	Train Driver Engine Room Rating (Merchant Navy) Lighthouse Keeper Air Traffic Control Assistant (D) Survey Sounder Shunter (British Rail) Aircraft Refueller Signal Operator (British Rail) Heavy Goods Vehicle Driver Bus/Coach Driver Taxi Driver Coast Guard (X) Fireman/woman (X)	Air Traffic Engineer Flight Engineer Merchant Navy Deck Officer Traffic Assistant (British Rail) Traffic Manager (B) Dock Foreman/woman Foreman/woman (Marshalling Yard – British Rail) Movements Inspector Foreman/Woman (Earth-moving and Civil Engineering Equipment Operating Occupations) Port Control Signalman/woman Merchant Navy Engineering Officer (M) Merchant Navy Radio Officer	Airline Pilot Test Pilot, Aircraft Flying Instructor (U) Flight Navigator Pilot (Ship) Master (Foreign-Going Ship) Helicopter Pilot Hovercraft Pilot Air Traffic Control Officer (D)
M Engineering Processing & other Applied Technologies	Machine Tool Operator Packer Paper Mill Worker Clothing Production Worker Food Packer Garment Examiner Sewing Machine Operator Glass Lathe Worker Brickmaker Offset Duplicating Machine Operator Cine-Film Processing Cutting and Assembling Worker Cutter (Garments) Product Finisher Warp Spinning Machine Operator Cigarette Making Machine Operator Band Knife Operator	Aircraft Maintenance Engineer Automatic Lathe Setter Capstan Setter/Operator Plater Engineering Inspector Fitter (Jig and Tool) Flight Engineer Machine Tool Setter Metal Spinner Die Miller Plate-maker (Printing) Precision Grinder Sheet Metal Worker Textile Weaver Wallpaper Printer Cutting Machinist Pneumatics and Hydraulics Fitter Miner Printer	Foreman/woman in Making and Repairing Occupations eg: glassworking, clay and stoneworking, printing and photographic processing, book binding, paperworking, paperboard products, textile materials, leather working, rubber and plastics, metal and electrical products and related coating operations. Colliery Official Reprographic Technician Signals and Telecommunications Technician Mining Surveyor Printing Machine Manager Industrial Radiographer Quality Control Inspector	Control Engineer Drilling Engineer Electrical Engineer Mechanical Engineer Production Engineer Biomedical Engineer (N) Chemical Engineer Quarry Manager (B) Naval Architect Nuclear Engineer (N) Printing Technologist Textile Technologist Ceramics Technologist Colour Technologist Food Scientist/Technologist (N) Fuel Technologist Glass Technologist Leather Technologist Packing Technologist

Remember the Watch Point

The distinction by occupational level is adapted from the classification used in 'Job Ideas', Careers and Occupational Information Centre, 1982; also with reference to Standard Occupational Classification HMSO 1990.

JOB FAMILY	LEVEL 1	LEVEL 2	LEVEL 3	LEVEL 4
	Unskilled and semiskilled jobs. These usually need no specific educational qualifications. Practical abilities are more important.	Skilled practical and clerical jobs. These usually involve greater on-the-job training and may require some passes at GCSE/S grade.	Supervisory and middle management, technician and some professional occupations come into this category. Occupations in this group usually require at least GCSE/S grade (A–C/1–3) and often A levels/H grade passes. Completion of some further training – often full-time – is usually necessary.	Professional and higher management occupations. Entry to these occupations usually requires the successful completion of a recognised degree or diploma course or extensive experience and highly developed skills at an equivalent level. Postgraduate training is often desirable.
	Woodworking Machinist Electronic Bench Tester Assembler Chemical Plant Operative Tyre/Exhaust Fitter Oil Drilling Production Worker Engineering Machine Operator	Engineering Instructor Compositor (Printing; Typesetter Electrical Fitter Mining Engineering Craftsman/woman Patternmaker (Foundry) Quality Control Assistant Electronic and Circuit Inspector Carpet Weaver Circular Machine Knitter Optical Slab Grinder and Polisher Glass Cutter (Decorations) Plaster Mould Maker (Pottery) Electrotyper Photographic Finisher Moulder/Core-Maker (Foundry) Wood Sawyer, Saw Doctor Dyer Printing Machine Manager Fabric Weaver Aero-Engine Fitter Agricultural Mechanic (J) Maintenance Fitter Contractors Plant Mechanic Roughneck (Oil Drilling) Auto Electrician Welder Motor Mechanic Theatrical Electrician (Q) Soundman/woman (Film/TV) (Q) Photographic Technician (S) Technician – Education (J)	Quarry Manager (B) Toolpusher (Oil Drilling) Driller (Oil Drilling) Derrickman (Oil Drilling) Production Manager (B) Technical Author (N&R) Film Cameraman/woman (Q) Soundman/woman (Film/TV) (Q) Merchant Navy Engineering Officer (L)	Paint Technologist Lighting Engineer Patent Examiner Hydrographic Surveyor Brewer Energy Technologist and Environmental Engineer Computer Engineer Ergonomist Water Engineer Petroleum Engineer Electronic Engineer Rubber Technologist Printing Technologist Polymer Technologist Mining Engineer Broadcasting Engineer Development Engineer Oil Drilling Rig Manager/Toolpusher Production Manager (B) Technical Author (N&R) The majority of these occupations will be relevant to job family N.

Remember the Watch Point

The distinction by occupational level is adapted from the classification used in 'Job Ideas', Careers and Occupational Information Centre, 1982; also with reference to Standard Occupational Classification HMSO 1990.

JOB FAMILY	LEVEL 1	LEVEL 2	LEVEL 3	LEVEL 4
	Unskilled and semiskilled jobs. These usually need no specific educational qualifications. Practical abilities are more important.	Skilled practical and clerical jobs. These usually involve greater on-the-job training and may require some passes at GCSE/S grade.	Supervisory and middle management, technician and some professional occupations come into this category. Occupations in this group usually require at least GCSE/S grade (A–C/1–3) and often A levels/H grade passes. Completion of some further training – often full-time – is usually necessary.	Professional and higher management occupations. Entry to these occupations usually requires the successful completion of a recognised degree or diploma course or extensive experience and highly developed skills at an equivalent level. Postgraduate training is often desirable.

CHART 4 NATURAL, SOCIAL & MEDICAL SCIENCES

JOB FAMILY	LEVEL 1	LEVEL 2	LEVEL 3	LEVEL 4
N Natural Sciences and Mathematics	Tracer/Drawing Office Assistant	Laboratory Technician (Educational Laboratories) Laboratory Technician (Industrial Laboratories) Cartographer (S) Ordnance Survey Technician Draughtsman/woman (S) Laboratory Assistant Technicians – Medicine & Medical Technologies (O)	Assistant Scientific Officer (Civil Service) Ordnance Survey Technician Statistics Officer Food Technologist Technical Author (R&M) Computer Programmer (D) Metallurgy Technologist Laboratory Technician (Educational Laboratories) Laboratory Technician (Industrial Laboratories) Technicians – Medicine & Medical Technologies (O) Radiographer (v)	Biologist (J) Biophysicist Geologist Microbiologist (O) Scientific Officer (Civil Service) (J) Chemist Public Analyst Astronomer Mathematician Metallurgist Meteorologist Physicist Statistician Forensic Scientist Taxonomist Ecologist (J) Mineralogist Oceanographer Archaeologist Minerals Surveyor Materials Scientist Bacteriologist Biochemist Scientific Journalist (R) Systems Analyst (D) Professional Scientist Food Scientist (M) Computer Programmer (D) Geophysicist Economist (D) Information Officer/Scientist (D) Systems Analyst (D) Botanist (J)

Remember the Watch Point

The distinction by occupational level is adapted from the classification used in 'Job Ideas', Careers and Occupational Information Centre, 1982; also with reference to Standard Occupational Classification HMSO 1990.

JOB FAMILY	LEVEL 1	LEVEL 2	LEVEL 3	LEVEL 4
	Unskilled and semiskilled jobs. These usually need no specific educational qualifications. Practical abilities are more important.	Skilled practical and clerical jobs. These usually involve greater on-the-job training and may require some passes at GCSE/S grade.	Supervisory and middle management, technician and some professional occupations come into this category. Occupations in this group usually require at least GCSE/S grade (A–C/1–3) and often A levels/H grade passes. Completion of some further training – often full-time – is usually necessary.	Professional and higher management occupations. Entry to these occupations usually requires the successful completion of a recognised degree or diploma course or extensive experience and highly developed skills at an equivalent level. Postgraduate training is often desirable.
				Veterinary Surgeon (J) Zoologist (J) Ornithologist (J) Marine Biologist (J) Soil Scientist (J) Surveyor (K) Structural Engineer (K) Civil Engineer (K) Nuclear Engineer (M) Biomedical Engineer (M) Technical Author (M&R) Dentist/Dental Surgeon (V) Medical Laboratory Scientist (O) Surgeon (O) Engineers and Technologists
O Medicine and Medical Technologies	Sterile Supplies Worker (Hospital)	Medical Laboratory Technician (N) Medical Physics Technician (N) Physiological Measurement Technician (N) Carciological Technician (N) Electro-Encephalography Technician (N) Contact Lens Technician (N) Audiology Technician (N) Neurophysiology Technician (N) Dispensing Technician (Pharmacy) (N) Dental Technician (N) Medical Photographer (N)	Physiological Measurement Technician (N) Cardiological Technician (N) Electro-encephalography Technician (N) Contact Lens Technician (N) Audiology Technician (N) Neurophysiology Technician (N) Diagnostic and Therapeutic Radiographer Medical Laboratory Technician (N) Medical Physics Technician (N)	Dispensing Optician Ophthalmic Optician Pathologist Pharmacist (Hospital) Pharmacologist Anaesthetist Radiologist Surgeon (N) Hospital Doctor Community Medical Officer (B) General Medical Practitioner Community Health Service Doctor Psychiatrist Orthoptist Retail Pharmacist (C) Medical Laboratory Scientist (N) Homeopathic Doctor/Homeopath Microbiologist (N)

Remember the Watch Point

The distinction by occupational level is adapted from the classification used in 'Job Ideas', Careers and Occupational Information Centre, 1982; also with reference to Standard Occupational Classification HMSO 1990.

JOB FAMILY	LEVEL 1	LEVEL 2	LEVEL 3	LEVEL 4:
	Unskilled and semiskilled jobs. These usually need no specific educational qualifications. Practical abilities are more important.	Skilled practical and clerical jobs. These usually involve greater on-the-job training and may require some passes at GCSE/S grade.	Supervisory and middle management, technician and some professional occupations come into this category. Occupations in this group usually require at least GCSE/S grade (A–C/1–3) and often A levels/H grade passes. Completion of some further training – often full-time – is usually necessary.	Professional and higher management occupations. Entry to these occupations usually requires the successful completion of a recognised degree or diploma course or extensive experience and highly developed skills at an equivalent level. Postgraduate training is often desirable.
P Social Sciences and Legal Services	Court Usher	Court Officer (D) Justices' Clerks Assistant (D) Barristers' Clerk Legal Secretary (D)	Senior Barristers' Clerk General Secretary (Trade Union) Legal Executive Court Reporter	Psychologist (Child, Clinical, Occupational) (V&U) Historian Political Scientist Sociologist Geographer Criminologist Judge Barrister/Advocate Solicitor Economist (E) Anthropologist Chief Executive (Local Authority) (B) Court Clerk Procurator Fiscal Crown Prosecutor Clerk to the Justices Probation Officers (U)

Remember the Watch Point

The distinction by occupational level is adapted from the classification used in 'Job Ideas', Careers and Occupational Information Centre, 1982; also with reference to Standard Occupational Classification HMSO 1990.

JOB FAMILY

	LEVEL 1	LEVEL 2	LEVEL 3	LEVEL 4
	Unskilled and semiskilled jobs. These usually need no specific educational qualifications. Practical abilities are more important.	Skilled practical and clerical jobs. These usually involve greater on-the-job training and may require some passes at GCSE/S grade.	Supervisory and middle management, technician and some professional occupations come into this category. Occupations in this group usually require at least GCSE/S grade (A–C/1–3) and often A levels/H grade passes. Completion of some further training – often full-time – is usually necessary.	Professional and higher management occupations. Entry to these occupations usually requires the successful completion of a recognised degree or diploma course or extensive experience and highly developed skills at an equivalent level. Postgraduate training is often desirable.

CHART 5   ARTS & MEDIA

JOB FAMILY	LEVEL 1	LEVEL 2	LEVEL 3	LEVEL 4
Q Performing Arts	Costume Assistant Wardrobe Assistant (TV) Dresser (Theatrical) Cinema Projectionist Stage Hand Floor Assistant – Broadcasting Fashion/Photographer's Model (A)	Session Musician Assistant Stage Manager Make-up Artist (S) Stage Carpenter (K) Film Assembler Acrobat Theatrical Electrician (M) Singer Musical Instrument Maker Dancer Production Assistant Conjurer Clown Choreographer (S) Actor/Actress Assistant Floor Manager Film Cameraman/woman (V) Soundman/woman (Film/TV) (M) Fashion/Photographer's Model (A)	Animator (Films) Session Musician Assistant Theatre Director Actor/Actress Announcer (TV, Radio) (T) Newsreader (TV, Radio) (T) Drama Coach Film Director Singer Dancer Music Teacher (U) Research (Broadcasting) Stage Manager Theatre Manager (B) Choreographer (S) Composer Orchestrator Arranger Assistant Director (Theatre/TV) (B) Casting Director (Film and Theatre) (B) Film Camera Man/woman (M) Dance Teacher (U) Floor/Studio Manager Soundman/woman (Film/TV) (M) Commentator (T) Producers/(Radio/TV) (B) Programme Organiser (TV/Radio) (T) Newsreader (T)	Orchestral Musician Director (Theatre) (B) Film Director Presenter (Broadcasting) Arts Administrator Conductor (Musical) Choreographer (S) Session Musician Composer Orchestrator Director (TV) (B) Casting Director (Film and Theatre) (B) Producer/(TV/Radio) (B) Art Director (Films) (S) Commentator (T) Senior Announcer (Radio/TV) (T) Programme Organiser (TV/Radio) (T) Music Therapist (v) Drama Therapist (v)

Remember the Watch Point

The distinction by occupational level is adapted from the classification used in 'Job Ideas', Careers and Occupational Information Centre, 1982; also with reference to Standard Occupational Classification HMSO 1990.

JOB FAMILY	LEVEL 1	LEVEL 2	LEVEL 3	LEVEL 4
	Unskilled and semiskilled jobs. These usually need no specific educational qualifications. Practical abilities are more important.	Skilled practical and clerical jobs. These usually involve greater on-the-job training and may require some passes at GCSE/S grade.	Supervisory and middle management, technician and some professional occupations come into this category. Occupations in this group usually require at least GCSE/S grade (A–C/1–3) and often A levels/H grade passes. Completion of some further training – often full-time – is usually necessary.	Professional and higher management occupations. Entry to these occupations usually requires the successful completion of a recognised degree or diploma course or extensive experience and highly developed skills at an equivalent level. Postgraduate training is often desirable.
R Literary	Novelist Poet Scriptwriter	Proof Reader Greetings Card Editor Magazine Writer (Freelance) Library Assistant (D) Bilingual Secretary (D) Novelist Poet Scriptwriter	Editor – Commissioning/Desk (Publishing) Editor (Newspaper) Interpreter Reviewer/Critic – Theatre/Restaurant/Books etc Translator Journalist – Newspaper/Magazine/Freelance Reader (Publishing) Editorial Assistant (Publishing) Advertising Copywriter (A) Technical Author (N&M) Reporter – Local/National Newspaper Proof Reader Playwright Scriptwriter Public Relations Officer (A) Reporters (Radio/TV) Sub Editor Ghost Writer Biographer Literary Agent (A) Travel Courier (W)	Playwright Scriptwriter Conference Interpreter Linguist (Translator/Interpreter) Senior Editor (Publishing) (A) Editor (Newspaper) Interpreter Translator Journalist Magazine Writer (Freelance) Reporter Librarian (D) Technical Author (N&M) Public Relations Officer (A) Reporter/(TV/Radio) Sub Editor Ghost Writer Biographer Scientific Journalist (N)
S Art and Design	Floristry Assistant (C) Display Assistant Cake Decorator (W)	Draughtsman/woman (N) Ceramics Painter Embroiderer Jewellery Engraver Industrial Photographer Leather Worker Lighting Designer Paste-up Artist Picture Restorer Pottery Worker Sign Writer Silversmith	Photo Journalist Technical Illustrator Architectural Technician (K) Footwear Designer Clothing Designer Fashion Designer Graphic Designer Press Photographer Portrait Photographer Set Designer (Theatre, Television) Interior Designer Industrial Designer	Landscape Architect (J) Fine Artist Clothing Designer Fashion Designer Graphic Designer/Illustrator Visualiser (Advertising) Interior Designer Industrial Designer Art Director (Advertising Agency) Art Therapist (V) Art Director (Films) (Q) Architect (K)

Remember the Watch Point

The distinction by occupational level is adapted from the classification used in 'Job Ideas', Careers and Occupational Information Centre, 1982; also with reference to Standard Occupational Classification HMSO 1990.

JOB FAMILY	LEVEL 1	LEVEL 2:	LEVEL 3:	LEVEL 4:
	Unskilled and semi skilled jobs. These usually need no specific educational qualifications. Practical abilities are more important.	Skilled practical and clerical jobs. These usually involve greater on-the-job training and may require some passes at GCSE/S grade.	Supervisory and middle management, technician and some professional occupations come into this category. Occupations in this group usually require at least GCSE/S grade (A–C/1–3) and often A levels/H grade passes. Completion of some further training – often full-time – is usually necessary.	Professional and higher management occupations. Entry to these occupations usually requires the successful completion of a recognised degree or diploma course or extensive experience and highly developed skills at an equivalent level. Postgraduate training is often desirable.
		Stencil/Screen Maker	Wallpaper Designer	Photographer
		Technician (Sculpture)	Industrial Photographer	Three Dimensional Designer
		Wallpaper Designer	Commercial Photographer	Footwear Designer
		Etcher, Engraver	Photographer	Textile Designer
		Bookbinder	Textile Designer	Town Planner (B)
		Photographer	Beauty Therapist (V&W)	Antique Dealer (C)
		Portrait Photographer	Sculptor	Choreographer (Q)
		Photographic Technician (M)	Silversmith	Museum/Art Gallery Curator (B)
		Hairdresser (W&C)	Antique Dealer (C)	
		Sculptor	Kitchen Planner (H)	
		Antique Dealer (C)	Choreographer (Q)	
		Florist (C)		
		Window Dresser/Display Assistant (C)		
		Antique Furniture Repairer (I)		
		Make Up Artist (Q)		
		Choreographer (Q)		
		Cordon Bleu Chef (W)		
		Wig Maker (H)		
		Upholsterer (I)		
		Tailor – Bespoke (H)		
		Dressmaker (H)		
		Cartographer (N)		
		Wrought-iron Smith (K)		

Remember the
Watch Point

The distinction by occupational level is adapted from the classification used in 'Job Ideas', Careers and Occupational Information Centre, 1982; also with reference to Standard Occupational Classification HMSO 1990.

JOB FAMILY	LEVEL 1	LEVEL 2	LEVEL 3	LEVEL 4:
	Unskilled and semiskilled jobs. These usually need no specific educational qualifications. Practical abilities are more important.	Skilled practical and clerical jobs. These usually involve greater on-the-job training and may require some passes at GCSE/S grade.	Supervisory and middle management, technician and some professional occupations come into this category. Occupations in this group usually require at least GCSE/S grade (A–C/1–3) and often A levels/H grade passes. Completion of some further training – often full-time – is usually necessary.	Professional and higher management occupations. Entry to these occupations usually requires the successful completion of a recognised degree or diploma course or extensive experience and highly developed skills at an equivalent level. Postgraduate training is often desirable.
T Popular Entertainment and Professional Sport	Cinema/Theatre Attendant Swimming Pool Attendant Sports Assistant Stablehand (J)	Puppeteer Impersonator Golf Green Keeper (J) Riding Instructor (J&U) Comedian Disc Jockey Ringmaster Stuntman/woman Professional Sportsman/woman: Team Sports: Soccer, Cricket, Basketball, Rugby League Individual Sports: Golf, Lawn Tennis, Boxing, Darts, Snooker, Wrestling, Cycling, Motorsports, Stuntman/woman, Racing Car Driver. Equestrian Rider/Jockey (J) Musician, Singer (Popular Music)	Touring Manager (Entertainment) (B) Sports Instructor/Coach Sports Official Team Manager (Sports and Games) (B) Announcer (Radio, TV) (Q) Commentator (Sports and Events) (Q) Newsreader (Q) Leisure & Recreation Manager (W)	Team Manager (Sports and Games) Senior Announcer (Radio, TV) (Q) Sports Instructor, Coach Commentator (Q) Programme Organiser (TV/Radio) (Q) Leisure & Recreation Manager (W)

Remember the Watch Point

The distinction by occupational level is adapted from the classification used in 'Job Ideas', Careers and Occupational Information Centre, 1982; also with reference to Standard Occupational Classification HMSO 1990.

JOB FAMILY	LEVEL 1	LEVEL 2:	LEVEL 3:	LEVEL 4:
	Unskilled and semiskilled jobs. These usually need no specific educational qualifications. Practical abilities are more important.	Skilled practical and clerical jobs. These usually involve greater on-the-job training and may require some passes at GCSE/S grade.	Supervisory and middle management, technician and some professional occupations come into this category. Occupations in this group usually require at least GCSE/S grade (A–C/1–3) and often A levels/H grade passes. Completion of some further training – often full-time – is usually necessary.	Professional and higher management occupations. Entry to these occupations usually requires the successful completion of a recognised degree or diploma course or extensive experience and highly developed skills at an equivalent level. Postgraduate training is often desirable.

CHART 6   SOCIAL, HEALTH & PERSONAL SERVICES

JOB FAMILY	LEVEL 1	LEVEL 2:	LEVEL 3:	LEVEL 4:
U Education and Social Services	Nursery Assistant Organiser of Clubs for the Disabled Playgroup Organiser Home Help (Social Services) Warden, Sheltered Accommodation Care Assistant (Residential & Non-Residential) Play Leader Classroom Assistant Childminder (W)	Day Care Centre Staff (Social Services) Community Centre Worker Education Welfare Officer Play Group Leader Social Work Assistant Nursery Nurse Visiting Officer DHSS Nanny (W) Supervisor (Youth Training & Employment Training) School Secretary (D) Technician – Education (M)	Organiser (Citizens Advice Bureau) Organising Secretary (Voluntary Organisation) (D) Community Development Officer Community Relations Officer Home Help Organiser Community Drama Worker Private Driving Instructor Road Safety Officer Tutor/Organiser WEA Safety Officer Adult Education Teacher Minister of Religion Housing Officer (D) NSPCC/RSSPC Inspector Supervisor (Youth Training & Employment Training) Private Employment Agency Consultant/Interviewer Disablement Resettlement Officer Instructor (Prison Service) Trainer (Private Sector) (B) Training Officer (B) Personnel Officer (B) Dance Teacher (Q) Home Economist (W) Mobility Instructor (Guide Dogs for the Blind) (J) Funeral Director (B) Riding Instructor (J&T)	Lecturer (University, Polytechnic, College of Further and/or Higher Education) Teacher (Primary, Secondary, Special Schools) Organiser (Citizens Advice Bureau) Education Officer (Museum & Art Galleries) Community Relations Officer Educational Psychologist (P) Careers Officer Adult Literacy Organiser Minister of Religion Medical Social Worker Youth & Community Worker Probation Officer (P) Field Social Worker Residential Social Worker Court Liaison Officer (Social Services) Home Teacher Teacher – Prison Service Trainer (Private Sector) (B) Education Administrator Education Advisor Private Employment Agency Consultant/Interviewer Training Manager (B) Personnel Manager (B) Health & Safety Inspector (H&D) Environmental Health Officer (D&H) Trading Standards Officer (H&D) Home Economist (W) Flying Instructor (L) Funeral Director (B)

Remember the Watch Point

The distinction by occupational level is adapted from the classification used in 'Job Ideas', Careers and Occupational Information Centre, 1982; also with reference to Standard Occupational Classification HMSO 1990.

JOB FAMILY	LEVEL 1	LEVEL 2:	LEVEL 3:	LEVEL 4:
	Unskilled and semiskilled jobs. These usually need no specific educational qualifications. Practical abilities are more important.	Skilled practical and clerical jobs. These usually involve greater on-the-job training and may require some passes at GCSE/S grade.	Supervisory and middle management, technician and some professional occupations come into this category. Occupations in this group usually require at least GCSE/S grade (A–C/1–3) and often A levels/H grade passes. Completion of some further training – often full-time – is usually necessary.	Professional and higher management occupations. Entry to these occupations usually requires the successful completion of a recognised degree or diploma course or extensive experience and highly developed skills at an equivalent level. Postgraduate training is often desirable.
V Nursing and Personal Care	Ward Orderly Nursing Auxiliary/Assistant Ambulance Driver Hospital Porter Occupational Therapist's Assistant	Dental Hygienist Dental Surgery Assistant Artificial Limb Fitter Ambulanceman/Woman Nurse: Hospital Ward Clerk (D) Medical Records Officer (D) Medical Secretary (D)	Radiographer (N) District and Community Nurse Occupational Health Nurse Nurse: Hospital & Midwife Dental Technician Play Therapist Beauty Therapist (W&S) Health Visitor	Dentist/Dental Surgeon (N) Dietitian Orthoptist Principal Nursing Officer (B) Clinical Psychologist (P) Chiropodist Speech Therapist Health Visitor Physiotherapist Occupational Therapist Dispensing Optician Remedial Gymnast Art Therapist (S) Music Therapist (Q) Drama Therapist (Q)
W Catering and Personal Services	Waiter/ress (C) Porter/Hotel Porter (H) Barman/Woman (C) Canteen Assistant Kitchen Assistant Holiday Camp Staff Hostel Assistant Hotel Room Attendant Valet Maid Kitchen Porter Sleeping Car Attendant (H) Caretaker (H) Cleaner/Domestic (H) Chimney Sweep (H) Lift Attendant (H) Cloakroom Attendant Mothers' Help Counter Service Assistant (C) Linen Room Attendant (H) Window Cleaner (H) Trainee Butcher (C) Cake Decorator (S) Childminder (U)	Air Steward/Stewardess (C) Cordon Bleu Chef (S) Cook School Meals Supervisor Butler Waiter Chief Steward Head Barman/Woman Carver Club Steward/ess Hotel Receptionist (D) Beauty Consultant (C) Hairdresser (C&S) Masseur/se Cosmetic Electrolysist Manicurist Pedicurist Tourist Information Officer (A) Housekeeper Publican/Bar Manager (C) Warden/Hostel Warden Butcher (C) Nanny (U)	Purser Housekeeper Home Service Adviser Leisure and Recreation Manager (T) Hotel Manager Publican/Bar Manager (C) Institutional Manager Home Economist (U) Travel Courier (R) Tourist Information Officer (A) Restaurant/Catering Manager Warden/Hostel Warden Beauty Therapist (V&S) Fast Food Manager (C) Head Waiter	Home Economist (U) Hotel Manager Leisure and Recreation Manager (T) Institutional Manager Restaurant/Catering Manager

Remember the Watch Point

The distinction by occupational level is adapted from the classification used in 'Job Ideas', Careers and Occupational Information Centre, 1982; also with reference to Standard Occupational Classification HMSO 1990.

JOB FAMILY	LEVEL 1	LEVEL 2:	LEVEL 3:	LEVEL 4:
	Unskilled and semiskilled jobs. These usually need no specific educational qualifications. Practical abilities are more important.	Skilled practical and clerical jobs. These usually involve greater or-the-job training and may require some passes at GCSE/S grade.	Supervisory and middle management, technician and some professional occupations come into this category. Occupations in this group usually require at least GCSE/S grade (A–C/1–3) and often A levels/H grade passes. Completion of some further training – often full-time – is usually necessary.	Professional and higher management occupations. Entry to these occupations usually requires the successful completion of a recognised degree or diploma course or extensive experience and highly developed skills at an equivalent level. Postgraduate training is often desirable.
X Security and Protective Services	School Crossing Attendant Security Guard Traffic Warden Private Detective Gate Keeper Park Keeper Estate Ranger Member of Armed Forces (Non-Commissioned)	Dog Handler (J) Police Officer Fireman/Woman (L) Dock Policeman/woman Prison Officer Fire Prevention Officer Non-Commissioned Officer Coastguard (L) County Court Bailiff Customs Officer Member of Armed Forces (Non-Commissioned) Security Officer/Guard Railway Police Airport Police Private Detective	Assistant Prison Governor Armed Forces, Commissioned Service Non-Commissioned Officer Customs Officer Police Officer Assistant Chief Fire Officer Railway Policeman/woman Airport Policeman/woman Immigration Officer	Prison Governor (B) Chief Constable (B) Chief Security Officer (Private Undertaking) (B) Chief Fire Officer (B)

Remember the
Watch Point

173

The distinction by occupational level is adapted from the classification used in 'Job Ideas', Careers and Occupational Information Centre, 1982; also with reference to Standard Occupational Classification HMSO 1990.

APPENDIX 2 consists of the 6 OCCUPATIONAL INTEREST GROUPS – practical, investigative, artistic, social, enterprising, organisational/administrative, also referred to in WHO AM I?

OCCUPATIONAL INTEREST GROUPS

The occupations here include representative examples from a comprehensive range of occupations available in the UK. Based on the "World of Employment Map" they are classified under the following Code letters:

P – Practical
I – Investigative
A – Artistic
S – Social
E – Enterprising
O – Organisational/Administrative

Practical Occupations include skilled trades, technical and some service occupations, which involve physical co-ordination or strength, using and repairing machinery and understanding mechnical principles or exploiting natural resources.

Investigative Occupations include scientific and some technical occupations, which involve an interest in how and why things work or happen, and interest in discovering the facts of a situation, analysing and solving problems.

Artistic Occupations include visual and performing arts; design and literary occupations.

Social Occupations include educational and social welfare; occupations which involve advising, understanding and helping others with their problems.

Enterprising Occupations include managerial, sales, financial and service occupations, which involve an interest in managing, leading, negotlating with others or promoting projects.

Organisational/Administrative Occupations include office and clerical occupations, public administration and security, and involve interest in directing or organising procedures by means of paper work.

The three letter Code provides descriptions of occupations. For example, a Code of ESO for Sales Manager means sales management offers a lot to people with "enterprising" interests; something for people with "Social" interests and a little Organisational/ Administrative interest. In this way, the Codes provide a brief summary of what an occupation is like by showing its degrees of resemblance to the three major occupational groups which offer scope for these interests.

Watch Point

- Not every combination of letters has a list of occupations. For example, if you have ISE you will not find a list of occupations. You then look up the nearest combinations – IES, SIE, EIS.

- Don't worry if the occupations listed under your letters really do not appeal. Ask yourself what it says about your interests, e.g. if car sales does not fit for you, how about computer sales?

PRACTICAL OCCUPATIONS

WEM REFERENCE	JOB FAMILY	OCCUPATION
		PIA
6	I	Motor vehicle body repairer/sprayer
7	M	Printer-compositor
6	H	Document repairer
6	I	Piano repairer
7	M	Wallpaper printer
8	N	Tracer/drawing office assistant
8	N	Cartographic draughtsperson
6	K	Planning technician (construction)
10	Q	Stagehand
1	C	Shopfitter
10	Q	Theatrical electrician
10	Q	Stage carpenter
10	S	Architectural technician
10	S	Bookbinder
10	S	Stencil/screen maker
8	N	Photographic technician
		PIS
3	W	Beauty Therapist
3	W	Cosmetic electrolysist
12	V	Dental hygienienst
12	V	Remedial gymnast
3	W	Home economist
6	I	Radio and TV servicing
6	J	Animal nurse
6	I	Camera repairer
		PIE
7	M	Band knife operator
7	M	Printer
7	M	Chemical plant operative
6	J	Tree surgeon
7	M	Machine tool operator
7	M	Agricultural mechanic
6	K	Boat builder
6	K	Plumber
7	M	Patternmaker
7	M	Printing machine manager
6	I	Telephone engineer
6	K	Site manager, construction
7	M	Capstan setter/operator
6	J	Forest worker
6	K	Auto electrician
12	O	Dental technician
6	I	Watch and clock repairer
6	I	Upholsterer
7	M	Die miller
6	I	Telephone technician
		PIO
8	N	Laboratory technician
5	F	Telex operator
5	F	Card punching machine operator
5	F	Addressograph operator
6	K	Clerk of Works
6	J	Hatchery manager (fish farm)
6	J	Farm manager
		PSE
1	A	Driver/Salesperson, i.e. ice cream, hot-dogs, etc.
1	C	Reception engineer (garage)
6	H	Bus conductor
3	W	Canteen assistant
3	W	Mothers' help

WEM REFERENCE	JOB FAMILY	OCCUPATION
		PSE continued
3	W	Room service staff
3	W	Waiter/ress
6	H	Guard, British Rail
1	C	Petrol pump attendant
12	T	Riding instructor
6	L	Bus driver
6	H	Undertaker/Embalmer
12	T	Sports assistant
6	H	Patrol man/woman (AA/RAC)
3	W	Cleaner
4	X	Dog handler
5	G	Taxi driver
10	Q	Cinema projectionist
6	K	Fence erector
		PSO
4	X	Mobile security patrol man/woman
5	F	Telephone operator
12	U	Home help, social services
3	W	Hostel assistant
12	V	Nursing auxiliary
12	U	Teacher/craft and design technology
4	X	Coastguard
		PEO
6	J	Farm worker
6	J	Hatchery worker
6	L	Tractor driver
1	C	Shelf filler
7	M	Food packer
5	F	Office machinery operator
6	J	Horticultural worker
6	J	Groundsman/woman
6	K	Demolition worker
7	M	Garment cutter
6	J	Nurseryman/woman
7	M	Sewing machine operator
7	M	Assembly worker
7	M	Moulder/core maker
6	H	Bill poster
7	M	Wood sawyer
6	H	TV aerial erector
7	M	Packer
6	L	Crane driver
6	K	Construction plant fitter
7	M	Woodworking machinist
7	M	Sheet metal worker
7	M	Saw doctor
6	L	Dumper driver
		PAI
10	Q	Wardrobe assistant/TV dresser
10	S	Display assistant
10	S	Cake decorator
6	H	Picture framer
10	S	Window dresser
10	Q	Musical instrument maker
6	K	Painter and decorator
10	S	Silversmith
10	S	Floristry Assistant
3	W	Chef
6	H	Wig maker
6	H	Dressmaker
10	Q	Film assembler
10	S	Embroiderer
3	W	Hairdresser
10	S	Sign writer
6	H	Milliner
10	S	Technician (sculpture)
6	I	Musical instrument repairer
		PSI
6	H	Appliance demonstrator
3	W	Home service adviser
12	V	Ambulance driver
12	V	Hospital porter
4	X	Fireman/woman
6	J	Groom
12	V	Artificial limb fitter
		PEI
6	H	Tailor
6	I	Thatcher
6	H	Saddler
7	M	Quality control assistant
7	M	Electronic circuit inspector
7	M	Fault finder (electronics)
7	M	Engineering instructor
6	H	Taxidermist
6	J	Cowman/woman
6	J	Kennel hand
6	J	Stable hand
6	J	Poultry farm manager
		POI
6	K	Technical assistant (housing – Local Government)
6	H	Driving examiner
6	J	Game keeper
		PES
6	L	Deck officer (Merchant Navy)
6	J	Zoo keeper
6	K	Gas fitter
6	H	Car park attendant
12	T	Jockey
6	I	Domestic appliance serviceman/woman
6	K	Roofer
6	L	Lock gate keeper
6	J	Farrier
6	K	Carpenter
6	H	Lino fitter
6	K	Plasterer
		POS
6	H	School caretaker
3	W	Housekeeper
3	W	Kitchen assistant
12	O	Sterile supply worker, hospital
		POE
5	G	Engineer/storekeeper
7	M	Colliery official
12	T	Golf green keeper

INVESTIGATIVE OCCUPATIONS

WEM REFERENCE	JOB FAMILY	OCCUPATION
		ISP
12	V	Chiropodist
12	V	Chiropractor
12	V	Physiotherapist
12	O	Ophthalmic optician
12	V	Orthoptist
12	V	Osteopath
12	O	Surgeon
12	V	Homeopath

WEM REFERENCE	JOB FAMILY	OCCUPATION
		IEO
7	M	Quality control inspector
5	F	Computer programmer
2	B	Organisation and methods officer
8	N	Information scientist
2	B	Laundry and dry cleaning manager
2	B	Work study officer
8	N	Systems analyst
		IEP
7	M	Chemical engineer
6	K	Civil engineer
7	M	Control engineer
7	M	Drilling engineer (oil and gas)
7	M	Electronic engineer
7	M	Energy technologist
7	M	Biomedical engineer
7	M	Brewer
7	M	Rubber technologist
6	K	Structural engineer
7	M	Polymer technologist
7	M	Fuel technologist
7	M	Packing technologist
7	M	Nuclear engineer
7	M	Mechanical engineer
7	M	Food scientist/technologist
8	N	Minerals surveyor
7	M	Mining engineer
7	M	Timber technologist
7	M	Textile technologist
8	N	Geologist
6	J	Forest officer
6	K	Hydrographics surveyor
6	J	Zoologist
		ISA
2	B	Museum curator
10	Q	Researcher (broadcasting)
2	B	Town planner
		IES
12	V	Dispensing optician
7	M	Environmental engineer
1	C	Retail pharmacist
		ISO
7	M	Water engineer
6	H	Environmental health officer
6	H	Factory inspector
8	N	Public analyst
12	V	Dietician
		IPE
7	M	Petroleum engineer
6	L	Air traffic engineer
6	I	Fire/burglar alarm engineer
7	M	Instrument mechanic
7	M	Signal and communication technician
7	M	Numerical control machine maintenance mechanic
6	I	Refrigeration and air conditioning service mechanic
6	K	Surveyor
		IAS
6	K	Conservation officer and restorer (museum)
10	S	Landscape architect

WEM REFERENCE	JOB FAMILY	OCCUPATION
		IAP
7	M	Broadcasting engineer
10	S	Architect
		IOP
8	N	Materials scientist
8	N	Meteorologist
8	N	Metallurgist
8	N	Bacteriologist
8	N	Biochemist
8	N	Biologist
6	J	Botanist
8	N	Geophysicist
8	N	Astronomer
8	N	Physicist
8	N	Chemist
8	N	Archaeologist
9	P	Psychologist
6	H	Patent agent
7	M	Naval architect
		IPA
7	M	Dyer
10	S	Industrial photographer
7	M	Reprographic technician
7	M	Colour technologist
7	M	Printing technologist
7	M	Ceramics technologist
7	M	Glass technologist
7	M	Leather technologist
7	M	Lighting engineer
7	M	Paint technologist
		IPO
7	M	Patent examiner
7	M	Industrial radiographer
6	L	Air traffic control officer
6	L	Radio officer (Merchant Navy)
6	H	Technical assistant (public health office)
12	O	Dispensing technician, pharmacy
8	N	Biology technician
7	M	Metallurgy technician
7	M	Ergonomist
8	N	Forensic scientist
		IPS
12	O	Audiology technician
6	H	Pest control officer
12	O	Neurophysiology technician
6	J	Veterinary surgeon
12	O	Acupuncturist
12	V	Dentist
12	O	Cardiological technician
12	O	Medical laboratory technician
12	O	Medical physics technician
12	V	Radiographer
8	N	Assistant scientific officer/scientific officer (civil service)
12	O	Anaesthetist

ARTISTIC OCCUPATIONS

WEM REFERENCE	JOB FAMILY	OCCUPATION
		ASE
11	R	Author
10	Q	Drama coach/drama teacher
10	Q	Singer
11	R	Dancer
		ASI
10	Q	Music teacher
11	R	Reviewer/critic
10	S	Art therapist
		AIE
10	S	Commercial photographer
10	S	Photo journalist
10	S	Draughts person
10	S	Graphic designer
10	S	Footwear designer
6	H	Kitchen planner
10	S	Visualiser (advertising)
10	Q	Film animator
10	S	Fashion designer
10	S	Costume designer
		AIP
10	Q	Film cameraman/woman
6	H	Piano tuner
6	K	Wrought iron smith
6	I	Antique furnisher repairer
10	S	Ceramic painter
10	S	Lighting designer
10	S	Picture restorer
10	S	Wallpaper designer
		AES
6	H	Model
10	Q	Theatre director
10	Q	TV director
		AIS
10	S	Technical illustrator
10	Q	Actor/Actress
10	Q	Composer
11	R	Editor (Publishing/Newspaper)
11	R	Playwright

SOCIAL OCCUPATIONS

WEM REFERENCE	JOB FAMILY	OCCUPATION
		SEO
12	U	Minister of religion
12	U	Education welfare officer
12	U	Social work assistant
12	U	Social field worker
12	U	Careers officer
		SEP
12	U	Community centre warden
12	U	Youth and community worker
12	U	Warden, sheltered accommodation.
		SEI
12	U	Tutor/organiser (WEA)

WEM REFERENCE	JOB FAMILY	OCCUPATION
		SEA
12	U	Adult literacy organiser
		SPI
12	U	Nursery nurse
12	V	Hospital nurse
		SPO
2	B	Sheltered workshop supervisor
12	U	Residential social worker
12	U	Day care centre staff, social services
		SIA
12	V	Occupational therapist
12	V	Speech therapist
		SIO
12	V	Psychiatrist
12	U	Community relations worker
12	U	Medical social worker
12	U	Community development officer
9	P	Psychologist
9	P	Sociologist.
		SOE
12	U	Visiting officer DHSS
12	U	Road safety officer
4	D	Clerk, social/health services
12	U	Organiser, citizens advice bureau
4	X	Dock police
4	X	Assistant prison governor
12	U	Probation officer
12	U	NSPCC/RSSPCC inspector
		SPE
12	V	District nurse
12	V	Health visitor
		SIE
12	U	Director social services
12	U	Adult education teacher
		SAE
12	U	Community drama worker
12	V	Play therapist
12	U	Play leader
		SOP
12	U	Organiser of clubs for the disabled
		SAI
12	U	Play group organiser
12	U	Nursery school teacher

ENTERPRISING OCCUPATIONS

EAP

WEM REFERENCE	JOB FAMILY	OCCUPATION
1	C	Antique dealer
1	C	Musical instrument sales
10	S	Art director, advertising agency

EPI

WEM REFERENCE	JOB FAMILY	OCCUPATION
1	C	Sales assistant: electrical goods / DIY / car accessories etc.
6	J	Market garden manager
1	A	Car rental sales agent

ESO

WEM REFERENCE	JOB FAMILY	OCCUPATION
3	W	Courier
1	A	Publicity officer
2	B	Bingo club manager
2	R	Personnel manager
6	H	Tour operator
12	T	Cinema/Theatre attendant
3	W	Hotel receptionist
2	B	Betting shop manager

EIO

WEM REFERENCE	JOB FAMILY	OCCUPATION
3	F	Banker
1	A	Commodity broker
2	B	Land agent
2	B	Traffic manager
2	B	Contract manager
7	M	Quarry manager
11	R	Reader (publishing)
3	E	Wages manager
5	G	Transport manager
1	C	Retail manager
1	A	Advertising account executive
2	B	Training officer
5	G	Wholesale distribution manager
2	B	Purchasing officer
3	E	Stock broker's clerk
10	Q	Casting director, films/theatre
4	X	Armed forces, commissioned service

ESI

WEM REFERENCE	JOB FAMILY	OCCUPATION
1	A	Market research assistant
2	B	Party agent (political)
12	U	Educational service officer (museum)
12	T	Newsreader (radio, television)

EOI

WEM REFERENCE	JOB FAMILY	OCCUPATION
1	A	Telephone sales person
1	A	Credit club agent
4	X	Private detective
1	A	Marketing executive
1	A	Public relations officer
1	A	Senior editor (publishing)
1	A	Recruiting officer (Ministry of Defence)
1	C	Buyer

EOS

WEM REFERENCE	JOB FAMILY	OCCUPATION
4	D	Customer service clerk
1	A	Classified advertising sales agent
2	B	Appeals officer, charity
3	E	Building society manager
1	A	Sales representative
2	B	Housing manager
3	W	Institutional manager

EPO

WEM REFERENCE	JOB FAMILY	OCCUPATION
5	G	Motor cycle messenger
3	E	Cashier, petrol station

EIS

WEM REFERENCE	JOB FAMILY	OCCUPATION
1	A	Insurance agent
1	A	Sales negotiator (estate agency)
5	G	Ship and air broker
1	A	Car sales person
1	A	Auctioneer
1	A	Literary agent

EAS

WEM REFERENCE	JOB FAMILY	OCCUPATION
1	A	Market research interviewer
11	R	Advertising copywriter
11	R	TV writer
11	R	Translator
11	R	Journalist
1	C	Bookseller

EPS

WEM REFERENCE	JOB FAMILY	OCCUPATION
1	C	Supermarket assistant
1	A	Milk roundsmen/women

ESA

WEM REFERENCE	JOB FAMILY	OCCUPATION
11	R	Interpreter
2	B	Box office manager
2	B	Cinema manager
10	Q	Theatre manager

ESP

WEM REFERENCE	JOB FAMILY	OCCUPATION
3	W	Holiday camp staff
3	W	Recreation manager
4	X	Purser
3	W	Public house manager
3	W	Hotel manager
3	W	Institutional manager

ORGANISATIONAL/ADMINISTRATIVE OCCUPATIONS

OPI

WEM REFERENCE	JOB FAMILY	OCCUPATION
6	H	Meter reader
4	D	Audio typist
4	D	Shorthand typist
4	D	Typist
6	L	Traffic assistant (British Rail)
5	G	Storekeeper (engineering)
4	D	Filing clerk

OPS

WEM REFERENCE	JOB FAMILY	OCCUPATION
4	D	Medical secretary
4	X	Security guard, airport

OPE

WEM REFERENCE	JOB FAMILY	OCCUPATION
4	D	Farm secretary

WEM REFERENCE	JOB FAMILY	OCCUPATION

OIS

8	N	Research officer, social services
9	P	Solicitor
4	X	Traffic warden
6	H	Library assistant
4	D	Medical records officer
4	X	Customs officer
9	P	Legal executive
3	E	Tax officer
2	B	Local government administrator
9	P	Barristers clerk
9	P	Justices clerk
9	P	Law clerk

OIE

3	E	Actuary
3	E	Tax inspector
8	N	Statistics officer
5	G	Post room clerk
3	E	Accounts clerk
3	E	Building society clerk
3	E	Counter clerk, post office
3	E	Cost accountant

OSE

4	D	Travel agency clerk
4	D	Airline counter clerk
3	E	Pensions information officer
6	H	Pawnbroker
3	E	Settler (bookmaking)
2	B	Health service administrator
4	X	Chief constable

OSA

11	R	Court reporter
4	D	Bilingual secretary
11	R	Conference interpreter
10	Q	Arts administrator

OIP

8	N	Ordnance survey surveyor
2	B	Data preparation manager
6	H	Archivist

OSP

| 12 | U | Home help organiser |
| 12 | V | Nursing officer |

OEP

| 5 | G | Stock controller |
| 11 | R | Proof reader |

OSI

4	D	Clerical officer/assistant, civil service
4	D	Ward clerk
6	H	Optician's receptionist
3	E	Rent officer
9	P	Court officer
9	P	Usher to magistrates' court
6	H	Funeral director

OEI

5	G	Shipping clerk
5	G	Import/export clerk
3	E	Claims officer (insurance)
2	B	Company secretary
3	E	Accounting technician
3	E	Insurance underwriter

OES

5	G	Chartered clerk (air bookings)
3	E	Sales ledger clerk
2	B	Car hire manager

APPENDIX 3 LEISURE ACTIVITIES according to your interest groups.

There follows lists of leisure activities that correspond with your interests as measured by the questionnaire on page 64.

These lists suggest activities that might be of interest to you. It does not imply that you will have the necessary skills, only the motivation.

PRACTICAL

repairing or mending things
bike or horse riding
walking/hiking
camping
playing football, cricket, hockey, netball
making things like model aircraft, dresses, etc, using patterns or instruction kits
cooking
gardening
do-it-yourself
mountain climbing
ice-skating
roller-skating
aerobic dancing
skiing
skin diving/scuba diving
bicycling alone for exercise
working out in a gym
jogging alone
swimming
archery
training animals
hang-gliding, sky diving
carpentry
candle-making
wine-making
sewing

INVESTIGATIVE

developing and processing photos
reading books and magazines on scientific or technical subjects
observing, collecting, identifying such things as birds, animals, plants, fossils, shells, rocks etc.
visiting museums, scientific or technical displays
watching and listening to documentaries or "in-depth" reports on TV and radio
playing chess, draughts, bridge, scrabble, mastermind, or other games of skill
computer programming
genealogy
self-development
meditation
attending lectures

SOCIAL

visiting and working with the handicapped, old people, etc.
taking part in guides, scouts, youth groups, etc.
planning and giving parties
attending sports events, pop concerts, films etc, with a group of friends
helping to raise funds for a charity
working with young children in play groups, sunday schools, cubs, brownies etc.
activities with the family
massage
spending social time with friends, at pubs, dinner parties, restaurants
joining clubs or activities primarily for the social functions eg. church, choral group, political party, drama club
sailing with others
travelling with friends or in a group
playing games where winning is not important

ARTISTIC

playing a musical instrument or singing
writing short stories or poetry
sketching, drawing or painting
taking part in plays or musicals
craft work, e.g. pottery, weaving, knitting, jewellery making, macrame, etc.
visiting art galleries, exhibitions, plays or concerts
flower arranging
yoga
photography
gem polishing
interior decorating
restoring antiques
sculpting

ENTERPRISING

playing monopoly, backgammon, poker or other 'games of chance'
doing small jobs, such as gardening or car repair work for a fee
taking part in debates or making speeches
following politics in the newspaper or on radio or TV
being on a committee
earning money by selling things
games where winning is important – squash, tennis, badminton, soccer, rugby, snooker, darts, cards, bicycle and motor racing (if winning is not important – the interest will be more social)
winemaking to save money
entering craft work in competitions

ORGANISATIONAL/ADMINISTRATIVE

using typewriters, calculators, computers for record keeping
keeping detailed accounts or a careful diary
tidying up sheds, cupboards, drawers, etc.
keeping times and recording results at sporting events
collecting and cataloguing coins, stamps, photo albums, scrap books
calligraphy

The Mercury titles on the pages that follow may also be of interest. All Mercury books are available from booksellers or, in case of difficulty, from:

Mercury Books
Gold Arrow Publications Ltd
862 Garratt Lane
London SW17 0NB

Further details and the complete catalogue of Mercury business books are also available from the above address.

SUPER JOB SEARCH
The Complete Manual for Job-Seekers and Career-Changers

Peter K Studner

For the first time, here's a manual that has helped thousands of men and women learn the secrets behind a successful career change. Whether you are about to make your first job search or are in mid-career or even seeking to re-enter the job market after being away, Super Job Search will guide you through each step of the way to land the best of possible jobs. This seven-day programme will show you how to:

- Evaluate what you want to do and in what kind of environment.

- Organise your achievements to market your skills most effectively.

- Write a winning performance CV as well as the 20-second, functional and chronological CVs (includes 12 sample CVs).

- Discover *all* the places where jobs are to be found. How to get in touch with the *hidden job market*, write broadcast letters, answer advertisements, work with recruiters, network, maximize your time (includes 23 sample letters).

- Become a great networker, even if you have never done it before!

- Get interviews by telephone: latest techniques will show you the way.

- Interview, negotiate and set your personal action plan. Learn the six magic steps to a winning interview. How to control interviews. How to succeed at research, advice and direct interviews. How to get the salary you deserve.

Plus much more . . . including a chance to contact other Super Search users to expand your network and practise the techniques in *Super Job Search:* free to all who register.

'One of the most exhaustive guides on how to find a job . . . '*Korn/Ferry (world's largest executive recruiter)*

'This book makes finding the right job a proper marketing exercise just as *filling* the right job has become one for an employer. Both start with a rigorous review of who you are and what you can become.' — *Simon H. Barrow, Chief Executive, Charles Barker Human Resources.*

'In its comprehensiveness and clarity a must for the job-seeking executive. Perfectly timed to fill a growing need in our increasingly mobile employment environment.' – *Richard Cole, Managing Director, Charnos plc*

£9.99 (paperback)   **ISBN 1–85252–030–2**

HOW TO BE A WINNER

Nick Thornely and Dan Lees

Most of us want to be winners – which isn't too surprising as 'winners tend to be happier and more exciting than other people and, while they may or not be richer, their lives have a sparkle that losers can never experience'. Are you a winner? People in top jobs sound as if they should be winners but although presidents and monarchs hold the world's top jobs some of them have definitely not been winners.

  How to be a Winner shows how to identify the real winners: the winning president, the winning executive, the winning secretary or the winning doorman. It will also help you spot a winning company, a winning team or a winning country. Nick Thornley and Dan Lees – both winners in their very different ways – maintain that in the game of life, as opposed to sporting contests, everyone can be a winner and that a winning company, for example, should be staffed by winners from the newest recruit up to the chairman. Enjoyment, they maintain, is the key factor in developing the winning habit. If you are ambitious, enjoying what you do could take you right to where you can do the most good for yourself and your company while stress is strictly for losers.

  This amusing and thought-provoking look at the way we live and work will annoy the 'more than my job's worth' employee and the 'you're not here to think' type of employer, but the rest of us may well find that being a winner is more important than we realised. Winning – and helping other people to win – is what life is all about, all of which makes it essential to know *how to be a winner*.

'*Packed with confidence-boosting ideas*' . . . **Executive Development**

£6.99 (paperback)   **ISBN 1–85252–059–0**

COMMON-SENSE TIME MANAGEMENT

Barrie Pearson

Time management is vital because success requires more than doing tasks effectively and efficiently. Time must be found to persuade, motivate and influence people as well.

Fortunately, every person is given the same amount of time each day. Time is your most precious resource, and in this respect you are equal to the most successful people who have ever lived. Forget the idea that education and money determine success; they merely affect where you start from.

The crucial first step for you to take, however, is a conscious choice of the success you want. Then you need to believe you *will* achieve it and you must really *want* to achieve it. Action is essential to translate your vision and belief into reality.

This book is first and foremost about your own personal success. It spells out both the ingredients and action needed for you to achieve the success you want.

Using the techniques he has developed, Barrie Pearson has become an outstandingly successful management consultant and seminar speaker. He is Managing Director of Livingstone Fisher Plc, Management Consultants, London.

£14.95   **ISBN 1–85251–046–3**

LEAD TO SUCCEED

Michael Beer

When you are first promoted from the rank and file you can suddenly find yourself with a set of problems which you never had before and which you have no idea how to handle. These problems are almost all connected with *people*; managers find that they are expected to hire, train, supervise, motivate, discipline and sometimes fire the people on their team.

The problem is that the skills needed to achieve all this are not inherent or automatic; they must be learnt. Now, there are two ways of learning these skills. The first is by the seat of your pants, by slowly gaining experience on the job. The trouble with this method is that it is slow and it involves making mistakes along the way.

The second way is to watch others doing the job and to learn from their achievements – and from their mistakes. This way is what this book is all about. In these pages you will see how managers have handled the day-to-day people problems which cross every manager's desk. You will see the triumphs which they accomplish, and the disasters which they incur.

£5.99 (paperback)   **ISBN 1–85252–032–9**